Retirement

Retirement

*Coping with
Emotional
Upheavals*

Leland P. Bradford
Martha I. Bradford

Nelson-Hall nh Chicago

Library of Congress Cataloging in Publication Data

Bradford, Leland Powers, 1905-
    Retirement.

    Includes index.
    1. Retirement — Psychological aspects.   I. Bradford,
Martha I., joint author.   II. Title.
HQ1062.B72   301.43'5   79-4101
ISBN 0-88229-564-0 (cloth)
ISBN 0-88229-698-1 (paper)
Copyright © 1979 by Leland P. Bradford and Martha I. Bradford

Manufactured in the United States of America
    10   9   8   7   6   5   4   3   2   1

Contents

Dedicated
with great love
to our son
David Lee Bradford

Preface

When we retired we suddenly, surprisingly, shockingly discovered we had become part of an increasing minority group—Retired People—the old people.

The old people! Funny! We didn't feel old and we didn't feel different. We saw ourselves as we were before mandatory retirement caught up with us—physically vigorous, intellectually alert, socially active, capable of caring for ourselves, still able to make contributions in an active adult world. We definitely weren't aged and infirm.

It was as if we had suddenly been transported, like Dorothy in *The Wizard of Oz*, into a new world in which we were supposed to feel differently, act differently, to be different and passively rock away the declining years. But we just didn't feel old or "on the shelf."

However, we quickly began to feel social pressures to see ourselves as old. Magazines for retirees were filled with stories of those exceptional persons who had found active, rewarding tasks to keep themselves occupied—as if the vast majority of retirees submissively accepted a state of inertia. Our son called us, in a voice expressing new concern, to inquire how we were feeling now that WE WERE RE- TIRED. Our doctor, having read in the paper of some public accomplishment we had achieved, expressed pleasure that we had been so active. To our now-sensitive ears we heard only surprise that we, past our middle sixties, should be so active. Professional colleagues no longer sought our advice or informed us of new events and discoveries. We now belonged to the past. This was hard on our self-respect.

We felt pushed into a kind of psychological compound in which we were not supposed to feel a part of the vibrant, dynamic ongoing world. We imagined this socially contrived enclosure was expected to be a reward for past living and a method of mercifully treating "old" people.

We didn't like it for ourselves. Just being retired didn't make us old. Being retired, we felt, merely gave us more freedom to do other things. Someone said, "People are for living." We agreed. We wanted, and expected, much of the rest of our lives to be vibrant. We didn't want to be shoved aside.

We saw we had to resist within ourselves the social pressures that led to an aura of finality. We needed to close our ears to the comments some made, such as, "What do you expect at our age?" or, "After all, at our age," or, "You might as well make the most of it at our age." We realized we had to be as impervious as possible to avoid the effect upon us of those who had given in to retirement and complainingly waited for the end. We had to be aware of the insidious influence of the connotation of RETIREMENT that could produce apathy, depression and quiescence. We knew we should thoughtfully plan ways of coping with the necessary adjustments to retirement so we wouldn't fall into the trap of feeling and being old. Rather we needed to plan ways to make this new phase in life joyous, fulfilling and productive to us as individuals.

We recognized very quickly that retirement would make a difference in our marriage for good or ill, and that we would need to work on this problem.

But basically we came slowly to realize that the core of the adjustment to retirement lay in understanding and coping with the variety of emotional reactions caused by retirement.

Hence this book deals almost entirely with the emotional upheavals many, if not most, people encounter in retirement, and with the consequences of these emotional experiences on that period in life known as "The Elderly In Retirement."

The literature in this field deals far more with the obvious problems of selecting a retirement site, assuring financial security and developing hobbies to keep life interesting than it does with the basic and fundamental problems of the powerful emotional reactions, and their causes, that people encounter in retirement.

That is why the first part of this book describes how we unexpectedly encountered far more emotional reactions than we had anticipated—how we nearly sank into depression and discord under their weight—how we pulled ourselves together and found a way of identifying and coping with the emotions and their causes—and how the process both immeasurably strengthened the helpful companionship in our marriage and made it easier to meet future problems.

In this portion of the book we also give illustrations from conversations with other retired husbands and wives and from observations of other retired couples. Lest our friends and acquaintances believe that any incident related here refers to them, let it be understood that almost all stories told are a composite drawn from many conversations and observations.

Part 2 of the book draws on our professional knowledge and experience in the area of human relations in order to give background for the story of our experience. This section is not based on exhaustive reading in the literature on retirement nor on past research. It seemed best to us merely to tell the story of what one couple experienced and did at retirement.

A bit about our lives before retirement may give more meaning to the story of our experiences.

Leland, a trained psychologist, had a number of interrelated careers. Among them was teaching psychology at the University of Illinois, serving as the first director of adult education for the National Education Association, and, most importantly, co-founding and directing the National Training Laboratory in Group Development (now the NTL Institute of Applied Behavioral Science) from its inception in 1947 in Bethel, Maine, to his retirement in 1970.

The National Training Laboratory pioneered applied and basic research in group dynamics with training in human relations and thus sparked new methods of learning throughout much of the world: Sensitivity Training, Awareness Training, and many other methods, as well as encouraging the use of groups for a variety of individual and social problems.

Martha, although her field was not psychology, immediately became involved in the laboratory from its inception in 1947, first as a participant in many training groups and then serving in the important role of linking the laboratory to the community of Bethel, assisting in research, training wives and youth groups and counseling families attending the laboratory sessions. Thus she combined the role of housewife and mother with twenty-five years of deep involvement in almost all aspects of the laboratory process.

We hope this odyssey of our experiences in coping with the emotional booby traps of retirement will strike a kindred spark in others preparing for or experiencing retirement. We hope our story will be helpful to others in making this period in life growthful and fulfilling.

Part One

Defining the Problems

Introduction

We encountered three very fundamental, and potentially devastating, problem areas when we retired. Seldom considered before retirement, and with all too little written about them, these potential problem areas, like concealed booby traps, lie in wait for the unsuspecting and unprepared retiree and retired couple.

They are: the unexpectedly shocking and deep emotional reactions many feel as they retire; the many displacements, disengagements and losses accompanying retirement requiring replacement by satisfactory alternatives; and the need for a sensibly planned transition from one phase of living to another very different one.

Dealing with these three areas, long ignored, we found to be vital for an effective retirement. We witnessed again and again the tragedy of those overwhelmed and unable to cope with the internal turmoil they underwent.

It is not that these areas are necessarily disastrous or cause destructive results. Rather the extent to which they are recognized and the effectiveness with which they are handled determines whether the years of retirement will be happy, involving, growthful and self-rewarding or whether they will be unhappy, depressive and non-productive in terms of self-growth. Or so we found.

After we had unexpectedly and startlingly confronted these areas and painfully worked our way through the difficulties facing us and our emotional disturbances, we realized how unaware and unprepared so many persons are to encounter these crucial areas that lie at the heart of adjustment to retirement.

No matter how acutely an individual after long years in a career or with an organization is aware of approaching retirement—and may indeed be looking forward to it—when the moment arrives there may be a sinking feeling that something very important—even cru-

cially so—is suddenly, radically, surgically ending. Relief
phoria at the release from burdensome responsibilities or u
ing work may be engulfed in the painful realization that to
and all the tomorrows to follow—will include no job to go
ganization to be a part of, no colleagues with whom to share easy
comradeship. One will no longer belong and will, in fact, quickly become an outcast. The organization will move onward with scarcely a
ripple to mark the long years of effort one has made.

A termination to a major portion of life is occurring. What lies
ahead? These are thoughts difficult to deal with—thoughts laden
with painful emotions.

For those who have had positions of power, the power is suddenly
gone and the loss of accustomed power creates an emptiness that is
emotionally acute. For those who have had influence and prestige,
others come into the limelight. It is so easy when one retires to feel
unwanted, undervalued, disposable. Self-approval, self-respect and
sureness of identity can be easily shattered. This way lies self-doubt,
emotional stress, apathy and depression.

Even those who believe the hobbies planned, the travel dreamt
about, or participation in volunteer activities will pleasantly occupy
time, may find them less than fulfilling. The less than adequate satisfaction or the hectic efforts to fill hours may be the result. Disappointment can be followed by unhappiness and emotional
depression.

Housewives following their husbands to new places to live that are
satisfying to their husbands can feel betrayal, anger, hostility, loneliness, disruption from settled routines and loss of long-term friends.

Then there are those who have been so engrossed and narrow-fo-
cused in their work that they cannot emotionally accept retirement
and seek alternative ways of fulfilling their lives. For them retirement is to be dreaded and a horror to endure. Their emotional range
may extend from bitterness through apathy to depression. They live
out their years complainingly or nostalgically reliving the past.
Serenity and happiness is not theirs.

Marriages in retirement encounter in all too many instances deep,
lasting and destructive emotions for both partners. Prior to retirement such marriages are often endurable—but barely—because the
partners are separated through much of the day. Irritations felt by

each partner are not constant. Retirement brings closer living together and less escape from the causes of interpersonal tension. Irritations, hostilities and hurts, previously smoldering, now become active. The changes in patterns of living add to the irritations and hostility.

Couples who close the door to each other and who communicate by fighting, suffer continuing anger, even hate, perhaps mixed with feelings of guilt, punishment, pain, unhappiness, loneliness and the crushing of self-esteem. Of all the potential sources of emotional difficulty in retirement, unproductive marriages rate high.

Not infrequently the fear of poverty and destitution, even among those who have no cause for worry, creates anxiety, panic and abnormal penuriousness. These fears grow out of a belief in lowered marketability of resources and a deep worry about some unforeseen catastrophe. Whatever the reasons, strange behavior and debilitating emotions result.

Many, who in youth set high and often unattainable goals for themselves, are filled with a bitterness at retirement that eats away at them because their goals were not attained. The self is not always the target of the bitterness. Events, bad luck, prejudice, favoritism, enemies are rationalized as causes. Bitterness leads to envy of others, tendencies toward destructive actions toward others, unhappiness and depression.

Finally, for those who know not what to do with the time retirement brings, or who lack internal strength and security to seek new ways of living fully, boredom, that most dreaded of emotional reactions, results.

With our experience in professional work, we were well aware of the supreme importance of feelings and emotions in coping with unexpected change situations; in determining the fullness of living; in effecting the physical and mental state of the individual. We knew, also, that the depth of emotional reaction was frequently surprising and shocking to most individuals when the reaction occurred. We understood that emotional reactions may endure and not quickly pass away. We knew that emotions could continue to intensify and trigger deeper and more self-destructive ones—increasing hate, boredom, depression—resulting in stress on the physical being. Like the force of a tornado, a hurricane or a tidal wave starting from a small atmospheric disturbance, we knew that lesser emotional reactions inadequately dealt with lead quickly into more violent and destructive emotions. Often individuals are unaware of the slippage from lesser feelings to deeper emotions. Suddenly they are aware only of great anxiety or depression—not the build-up to these states. We knew, also, that feelings and emotions are very frequently multiple. Persons can feel frustrated, defeated, angry with themselves and others and expectant of future failure.

Frustration can lead into anger and punishment of self and others and into self-destructive actions.

Frustration can lead into hopelessness, despair, despondency, ineffective ways of dealing with problems, withdrawal, stress.

Boredom can lead to lowered self-esteem, anxiety, doubt of self, stress and functional illness.

Feeling unused and unwanted may lead to feeling undervalued, lowered self-worth, insecurity, inactivity or hyperactivity, reduced motivation, guilt, loneliness, an internal sense of emptiness.

All this we knew before we retired. We thought, therefore, that what emotional reactions we would experience we could easily handle. We didn't expect to be surprised.

We were wrong. Very wrong.

In spite of our past experiences, the emotional reactions each of us faced in retirement were far more varied, intense, disturbing and potentially destructive than we had ever expected. To our surprise, after our years of sharing work together, we discovered crucial areas of our relationship together that needed thorough exploration.

Suddenly cut off from professional work, from the organization we had helped to found, from working colleagues, from the excitement of daily problems, we felt lost, no longer wanted, disposable, expected to fade out of sight. This hurt—it hurt far more than anticipated. What new worlds should we attempt to discover? Or should we? Was retirement something to give into? As something disastrously and unhappily final?

New questions of who we now were raised serious and painful identity questions. The days were full of complaints about the ending of a career and about advice and counsel not being sought.

For Martha there was also the uprooting from a beloved home we had lived in for nearly twenty-five years in order to move to another part of the country. Her nest destroyed, the need to create a new one, the separation from long-time neighbors and friends and all, when she was not yet ready to make such a move, brought deeper emotional reactions than she had anticipated.

Then Leland's intrusion into the home during the day meant bumping into each other, irritations, needless overwork, duplication of effort. Tension mounted requiring careful readjustment of roles and relationships and setting of boundaries to allow needed privacy. Added to this were the deep emotional reactions and tensions each was struggling with, which inpinged upon the other and increased the difficulties each of us faced.

The first year of retirement brought us to a crisis. Martha brought the crisis to the surface and helped set the stage for us, working together, to seek solutions. One day she burst forth, "I'm tired of hearing about your lost identity and adjustment problems. How about mine? I've my own problems resulting from your retirement."

This shocked us both into the realization that we faced some very critical realities. We saw that we were falling victims to an avalanche of frightening and depressing emotions that would hurt our relationship as well as each of us individually.

We realized we could no longer drift. We saw we must work together to help each of us solve the problems we were confronting, and to make needed adjustments in our relationship so we could continue to share, work and grow together.

So, just as we had met other difficult periods in our lives, we confronted this most serious one that would affect the rest of our lives together. We talked, increasingly openly, honestly, without recriminations or defenses. For months over leisurely breakfasts, during afternoon teas, with cocktails before dinner, we explored our problems of changing from one phase of living with a complex set of problems, tasks, role responsibilities to an entirely new and different phase of living with an equally complex set of problems. In our talks, we cleaned out much of the debris of past misunderstandings and inadequate sensitivity. We built a new relationship for ourselves.

What was of tremendous importance to us was to experience the intensity and variation of emotional problems to be encountered in retirement. We had known about them theoretically before. In fact, Leland had occasionally given lectures on the "Psychology of Retirement." But he found he didn't really *know* about these emotional problems, however, until he had experienced them. *Now we knew that the many potentially deep emotional reactions, and the relations between husband and wife were the most crucial problems confronting those who are retiring.*

We observed other retired couples and we could sense in many cases that the relationships were strained. Other wives told Martha of troubles in relationships and understanding they were experiencing with their husbands. We observed some situations where marital stress seemed to be doing physical harm to one or both of the marital partners. Above all, we were impressed with the extent of parallel, non-sharing, non-communicating marriages.

The following three situations illustrate both some of the emotional and relational problems occurring in retirement and the lack of thought many persons give to such problems as they plan their retirements.

Various wives told Martha how lonely they felt moving at their age to another place and finding it difficult to make new, close friends. Some found the estrangement from old friends where they had lived, or from children, hard to bear. Even when they returned on visits, it was not the same. Neighborhoods changed. Friends dispersed. Children were involved in their own lives. So they swung between loneliness where they were now living and feelings of strangeness when they returned to the old home. Loneliness and the beginnings of depression were common.

We were shopping one day when we met a friend in the store. Always a placid person, her face was now flushed and she seemed disturbed. We inquired if anything was wrong. She burst forth, "I'm going crazy with Steve. I don't know what to do. He seems more insensitive than he's ever been to anyone else's feelings or wishes. Each morning he has the radio blaring until I think I'll go deaf. When I ask him if he will turn the volume down a bit, he says, 'Nonsense. You wouldn't get the full tone of all the instruments.' "

She continued to pour forth her problems. "As you know, we always go on a trip when he feels restless, whether I'm ready to go or not. I never thought retirement would be so awful. So disruptive."

We knew that giving advice is usually futile, but we did ask if she had let him know fully how she felt. She said every time she tried, a quarrel was the result. He argued her down and she was certain he hadn't really heard the expression of her feelings.

Recently we were having a leisurely breakfast with two old friends. They were within a year of retirement. He was a key executive in a world-wide company and the acknowledged expert on one aspect of the company's business. His wife told us how upset and angry he was feeling because a younger man, who knew half of what Paul did, was now being called upon to answer the technical questions Paul was more expert in answering.

We thought to ourselves that he was already suffering acutely an emotional reaction common to retirement. We knew it would get worse.

Later we talked about retirement and asked them what planning they were doing. Paul said he had two lawyers working on the most desirable trusts for their children. He had arranged separate safe-deposit boxes for him and his wife, and had organized his finances in the best possible way in the event of his death.

We asked what else they had planned. Mary, Paul's wife, said they were going to take a trip to the part of the country in which they had grown up to decide whether they wanted to buy a retirement place there.

We persisted and asked what else they had planned. They looked bewildered. Mary said *she* was looking forward to having more of Paul's time to herself. (We knew them both as strong, competent persons and we observed some signs of competition between them. We wondered what closer living would do to their relationship.)

When we mentioned a few of the potential emotional traps that could lie ahead, they admitted they hadn't thought about such possibilities.

The Displacements, Disengagements and Losses Occurring in Retirement

We expected some changes in our lives when we retired. There wouldn't be a daily job to go to and the long hours of activity our work had required. We would live in a different part of the country and in a new home. Would we like it? There would be opportunity for sports, hobbies, reading.

We weren't prepared, however, for the many displacements in the structure of our lives that had largely determined our behavior and the pattern of our living. We really hadn't realized the extent to which our lives had been carefully circumscribed by so great a number of seemingly small, but highly important, factors that went unrecognized at the time. They were just accepted parts of our lives, not to be thought about or questioned, like arising at a certain hour each morning because there was a job to go to.

Suddenly these elements—the scaffolding that supported and directed our lives—were lost or unneeded or different. We found ourselves surprisingly disengaged from a variety of life systems we had taken for granted. We were bewildered by the need to make so many readjustments or to find replacements. Our bewilderment carried a strong emotional loading.

For a while we tried to live our lives as we had before under the unspoken assumption that little had really changed. After all, we were the same two persons. But greater changes than we admitted had occurred and because the structure of our lives was different, we were different and so were our relations to one other. After hectic, but unsuccessful efforts to conform to now outmoded requirements, we finally realized that adjusting to these displacements and changes in our lives was indeed one of our crucial problems to solve in retirement.

By the end of a year we had identified over a dozen losses or disengagements requiring alternative structures and necessary changes in our attitudes toward ourselves. Making these changes took time and effort.

The Transition to Retirement

We knew we faced a transition in our living when we retired, but we didn't expect it to be so different from other transitions we had experienced—or so prolonged. We were wrong, again. We hadn't really counted on the depressing feeling that something very vital—the long years of Leland's professional career—with Martha's assistance—was ending, nor that, being as active as we might and rationalize as much as we could, we were on the downhill side of life. During the years that Leland was working professionally, even though some of his colleagues were younger, he didn't think of himself as being any different from them. Now, somehow, a line had been drawn between those who were inside and those outside. We were outside. During other transition periods there had always been a new position, a new challenge, a further opportunity to move forward. This transition was not the same. Gradually, profound changes in our lives from the habitual patterns and controls of work and home, developed over the long middle years of our lives, began to affect us. At first there was release from pressures, time for ourselves, a period to enjoy things we had had little time for before, the entrance into a leisurely, pleasant existence. Then the emotional impact of unexpected changes began to hit us. Some of the hobbies and events we had looked forward to were not quite as satisfying as we had anticipated. Slowly we found ourselves on a downward slide. The major transition turned out to be a series of breaks from the past not felt all at once.

As the euphoria of relief from demanding and often exhausting work disappeared under the onslaught of the many forces making us feel outside and no longer counted, we faced up to the realization that only the future is manageable, because the past is gone, and that we must meet directly and successfully the challenge of self-management and self-direction. If we were to have a future that was not despairing and depressing, we must actively create this future for ourselves.

We watched others struggle, sometimes successfully and often unsuccessfully, with the transition to retirement. We saw those who had won respect and admiration for their contributions in work apparently lost because they had no other interests. Some moved back to a previous home when one marital partner died, an indication that a full transition had not been made. We would observe men, newly retired, who maintained a pointless pace of frenetic activity because they were adjusted still to the work pace they had known before, and now didn't know how to find or create a new set of activities geared to a more reasonable pace of exertion. We found wives, separated by moving from friends of many years, sitting home-bound waiting for someone to approach them for friendship.

We realized that this most important transition period comes down, in the end, to the internal strength and motivation of the individual. Giving in to the feeling of finality—to hopelessness, to bitterness, to obsession with the downward side in life—is the way to depression, illness and death. We experienced ourselves how easy it would be to take this path and how difficult, how much thought, planning and energy was required to escape it.

We found that no matter the period in life, each individual must remain invested in life and living, must retain a continuing and vibrant connection with living, must remain emotionally attached to the on-goingness of life. To become a bystander invites personal disaster and untold pain to one's marital partner. We also found the need for each partner to work with and help the other.

The transition to retirement, necessarily lengthy because continuing changes occur, requires self-direction and self-management. To paraphrase former President Kennedy in his Inaugural Address: "Expect not that others will remake your life! Demand rather of yourself that you remake it to be emotionally, personally and socially alive and active!"

The response to this third important problem area in retirement carries the choice of continuing vibrant living or depressed withdrawal from life. Solving this problem requires both preparation throughout life, planning before retirement, and strong motivation and active effort after retirement.

Other Factors

One psychological adjustment some individuals face at retirement is to reject the ancient myth that all retired persons are "old". A growing majority are merely "elderly." The elderly are essentially healthy, vigorous, capable and potentially productive. The aged are mentally or physically infirm and no longer potentially active and productive. Chronological age is not the line of demarcation between the two groups. Reaction to retirement may help to determine which group the retired person enters. The elderly may have long years of relative good health before becoming really aged. Good mental attitudes and continuing socialization, spontaneity and ability and desire to cope with new situations aid the elderly from becoming aged.

It wasn't too long ago when most individuals didn't retire until physical or mental incompetence forced it upon them. Until the days of modern affluence most couldn't afford to retire. When they did, they usually remained part of the family structure, sitting near the fireplace warming ancient bones. Senior villages are modern institutions and the term "Senior Citizens" is a phrase most applicable to the present.

Another adjustment required in retirement is to the usually gradual process of aging. We find that each year we notice slightly less energy, a few things we no longer wish to do, and a few more aches. These, for us, are signals that we should find equally interesting alternative activities requiring less energy. We know all too well that they cannot be accepted as signs to seek the rocking chair to rock away empty hours. That way lies our entrance into the "aged" and the loss of our freedom and self-respect.

Thus our odyssey, to be described in future chapters, of our travails and efforts over the years of our retirement. From our experience we realize extremely clearly the necessity of preparing oneself throughout life for retirement. How one builds internal strength, gains ever-greater self-awareness, learns to cope with problems, rather than to be overcome by them, and seeks richness from living, has much to do with satisfactory adjustment to retirement. Our experience teaches us also the importance of continually developing, under changing circumstances, a marital relationship so that it can adapt in helpful ways to the changes retirement brings. We gained new meaning to our belief that a satisfying life can be built at any period in life. Now we know better the ways by which all this can be accomplished.

Chapter 1

Leland's Problems

Looking back I realize I approached retirement with a major feeling of relief and anticipation and only very minor apprehensions about any future problems. Certainly, I never foresaw the emotional consequences of the dozen changes, disengagements and losses retirement would bring.

I'm certain I dreamt during the last few years before retirement of not needing to go to the office each day to face a host of problems or bringing a briefcase full of work home at night. My mind would be relieved of constant thoughts and concerns about the organization which had become the major focus of my life. Tensions, worries and stress that seldom left me would be gone. The nagging doubts about some of my decisions would no longer be present. I would be free of tensions and emotional upsets. I could live leisurely with my mind cleared of problems and my emotions unruffled. Or so I dreamt.

For twenty-five years I had held the same top administrative position in the National Training Laboratories that I had helped to found. During the first decade of gaining recognition for a new field, the work, while difficult, had been thrilling and challenging. But the final few years before my retirement brought most of the problems of a growing bureaucracy, of rapid change and spread, of internal struggle and competition, of forces of disruption and disintegration within the organization. My position became more burdensome than enjoyable. I became overly sensitive to suspicions that some were waiting impatiently for me to retire after so long a tenure. I felt others saw me as a block to progress.

Whatever the reasons, my motivation was decidedly tipped toward retirement and my emotions toward release and relief. Hence, even with my professional training in psychology, I blocked out all thoughts of any negative feelings I might have upon retirement and instead fantasized a happy, carefree retirement period.

So, two years before I would be sixty-five, I urged the organization to plan for the succession to my position. A wide search was made. A year and a half before my retirement an ideal person was selected. I was pleased because I thought this would give us time for an orderly transition. I had visions of becoming an elder statesman with my advice being sought without my taking responsibility for any action. Unfortunately, shortly before retirement, circumstances made it impossible for the chosen person to fill my position. Another successor needed to be found quickly. The person selected had his own way to make and his own reputation to build. I was perceived as standing in the way. From the moment I retired, I promptly and abruptly became nonexistent in the organization. There were not even the ceremonies that might have attended my death. I was no longer considered. I was of the past. The phone in our new home in North Carolina never rang with calls from Washington.

This was change with a vengeance. Instead of relief and freedom, I felt deep hurt. After feeling important, valued, active, I now no longer felt needed and wanted. I felt that the many years I had spent in helping to build the organization were unappreciated. I even began to wonder if my professional reputation had been washed away by the mere act of retirement. I felt exceedingly sorry for myself.

Thus it was that I confronted the first of the dozen reconstructions and adjustments made necessary by retirement.

Coping with Changes in Transition

My first reaction to the hurt of oblivion was to strike back by proving in some way that I was not finished and that I could not be forgotten. I made an effort to secure a small grant for the organization. I received a sharp letter from my successor saying, in essence, that my help wasn't needed. Ruefully I realized he had to put his own stamp on the position I had held so long. Anything I did would only get in his way.

What else to do? During the depth of my feeling unwanted and of lessened value, one perceptive colleague told me, "Lee, don't worry. I have you lined up for seventy-two weeks of consulting next year." That helped. Knowing there are only fifty-two weeks in a year, his overstatement told me I was still valued and usable. I was not on the scrap heap. I was not aged. I was just a little older. So, for a while, I became involved in consulting with several organizations on their problems of development and change. This helped to prove to myself that just because I was retired my usefulness was not ended. However, I gradually became aware I was feeling the same pressures I had felt before: regular hours to go to work; efforts to succeed in the eyes of others; dreary hotel rooms and tasteless lonely dinners. I realized I was still being controlled by outside commitments.

This was the price I was paying to maintain my self-respect, to be listened to and to have influence, and to be active. On the other hand, I was relinquishing a sense of freedom and control over my life. Yet, I realized that having no reason to arise in the morning or facing empty hours would be disastrous.

During this period I became awakened to some of the dilemmas of retirement. (Some of the other eleven problems to be discussed later we discovered as time went on.) I saw that this transition period presented more difficulties, dilemmas and emotional disturbances than other transition periods I had experienced. The ending of a job once before, with a brief hiatus before assuming another position, had not filled me with worry at a younger age because I felt my knowledge and skills were marketable. Even enduring the Great Depression of the thirties with lowered income and job insecurity had brought no sense of hopelessness.

This transition was different in ways that struck deeply at my inner person. My feelings of being a non-person, of being unwanted and undervalued, and of blows to self-esteem clashed with needs to be less controlled by organizational requirements and with desires to do various things I wanted to do for myself. Surprisingly the routine of work built up over forty years of investment in a career left a stronger hold on me than I expected. Related to my retirement was the sudden change in social relationships. In the past these had been work connected. Many endured, though no longer connected to work. Occasional letters kept them alive. New relationships, no longer built on common colleagueship but now on personal grounds, needed to be created. My previous life investment in a career was no longer acceptable currency.

I thought of a person I knew. He had driven a bus along the same streets in a large city for most of his working life. He told others how tired he was of the monotony of his work and how anxious he was to retire. He moved south when he did retire, expecting a happy life. Instead, he missed driving his bus. He missed the familiarity of the route he had traveled each day. He recalled the pride he had in making his time schedule so people could count on arriving at their spot at a certain moment. Most particularly he missed the people who rode on his bus daily. Some he knew by name. He came to know the vicissitudes in the lives of some and he suffered with them. He had fantasies about his passengers and watched for cues in their moods and behavior to build on his fantasies. He began to realize how important his work had been in the lives of many. He realized he had had pride in his work. Nothing took its place for him. He didn't find situations in which he felt he had significance in other people's lives. He didn't try very hard. He lost his self-respect and was unhappy for the few remaining years he lived.

I found that coping with changes in the transition to retirement had a number of different dimensions, each carrying a heavy load of emotional reactions.

The first could be called "Looking Backward at One's Life." Forty years of a career! Were all my efforts, my energy, my absorption, my dedication to my work really worthwhile, or were they merely ways of passing the years and meeting family responsibilities? Was there even a ripple to mark accomplishments? What had my life been for?

I became aware of how crucially and emotionally different "Looking Backward" now was than at any other time in my life. I thought this must be so for almost everyone. Before, in the few instances I looked back, there was still the arena to stay in or re-enter. There were still new opportunities. "New breaks! Further changes." A work future!

But with retirement the arena had been left and opportunities for re-entrance slim. Now I was looking backward at a career and working life ended, and nothing could be done to change the past or recoup that area in the future. I could live on past memories and waste away my time, or I could build a new life, now self-oriented rather than work-oriented, but full of growth, self-rewarding, self-productive activities that create a richly meaningful new phase in life. I could be imaginative, innovative and pro-active about my life or I could molder in the doldrums and drink too much. The choice was mine.

I realized I was beginning to be morbid and self-pitying. I knew I had been fortunate in my life. I switched my thinking away from myself. I thought about the many, many persons whose work-life had been unhappy and disappointing or at best routine. How did they feel, now their years of formal working were ended? Falling short of early expectations, did they blame others, feel self-dislike, regret?

One evening I listened to a friend who, in the world's view, had had a successful life with position and authority and a good family life. He told me that while he had not been unhappy in his work-life, he hadn't really enjoyed it. The things he had wanted to do with his life hadn't been done. Twice, he said, he felt he had turned down opportunities he wished now he had taken. After that he was locked into family responsibilities. He wasn't crying or complaining. He just felt strongly that he had never reached his potential.

I thought of those whose lives were far less fortunate, whose jobs were monotonous and who really hated doing what they were doing, whose jobs had no status, no depth or meaning. How did they feel looking backward?

The second major emotional jolt for me in looking backward came as I watched the directions I had helped set radically changed, and accomplishments I thought I had achieved were eliminated in the organization which I had helped found and in which I had spent so many years. I suppose many persons who have struggled hard toward certain goals and now sat on the sidelines and watched these gains discarded felt as I did. I could say to myself that this was the way of life, that each person had a turn. Saying this, however, didn't eliminate the pain I felt nor stop the question of whether my efforts had not been futile. I found coping with the emotions raised by this situation one of my most difficult problems in transition.

On the other hand, "Looking Backward" was a tremendous learning experience that aided me to "Look Forward." I had time and desire to look more deeply at myself, to assess mistakes made, examine behavior I wished to change. Clearing out the past, now I could face the two alternatives mentioned earlier. I could start to build anew. Here was a great challenge and a difficult task. I felt my spirits rise.

The answer for me was to use some aspect of my background to maintain my self-respect without allowing myself to be placed in the pressure cooker of the trying demands I had known before. I needed to leave time for leisure, for myself, for hobbies and for other mundane affairs. I needed to plan a balanced life for myself that was still productive, but now self-rewarding. I wasn't going to fear or give in to retirement. I was going to make this new period fruitful.

I found the answer for myself in turning back to writing. I had done some writing from time to time and always had wanted to do more. Now I would write what I wanted at a pace that suited me. Publishing deadlines were no longer to control me.

What I learned about myself as I struggled from a settled, productive, controlled existence through an unsettled, disruptive period in which clear purpose and meaning were in question, no clear pathway to the future apparent, and ego blows painfully felt, should help me face the future. I had learned more fully to understand myself and my needs. I had begun to learn how to establish my own challenges set within my body limits. I had learned how deeply felt unexpected emotions could be, and I had succeeded in accepting and managing them. I had found harmony in myself and how to live with myself and find enjoyment from within me. I had less anxiety about the future and more peace in the present. I hoped I was better prepared to cope with whatever the future held.

I know each person enters retirement differently from others. Some seem to have no problems or emotional disturbances and fit into a new way of living with ease and enjoyment. Many remain active, stay vibrant and treasure living. Others live unhappy, inactive, unproductive, nongrowing, complaining existences. The differences are inward. They relate to earlier patterns of dependence on self or on others, knowledge or lack of knowledge of self, being and accepting oneself or endeavoring to live up to a false image, resistance to change or readiness to cope with change. Preparation for retirement largely lies in the way the person has constructed his life.

Many fight retirement in a variety of ways—by denying its eventuality until it arrives, by frenetically rushing at the same pace as before, by refusing to look at themselves and their behavior in this new phase. Needs for influence, status, power, authority, youth, beauty are hard to relinquish. When these needs are predominant, the retired individuals become unhappy, failing both to see themselves clearly and to cope with emotional jolts.

I found that the answer to the emotional problems of retirement was twofold: prepare for retirement by understanding as many of the emotional disturbances and their causes as one can and, throughout the years before retirement, become as conversant with oneself as possible. I found I must know myself. Be myself. The difficulty lay in learning enough about myself.

I remembered a couple of lines from a poem I had read many years before.

Some things one gets out of one's system
And other things in.

As I passed through this transitional struggle, I observed other men just retiring attempt the same struggle. Some seemed to have no problems. Some came through their struggles successfully. Others ended disastrously. Some tried to impress others with their past accomplishments. Others, using the methods of their working years, tried to direct the activities of others. Some gave up in despair and without dignity sank into depression.

As I experienced myself confronting the problems of adjustment to retirement, I became both aware of and astounded at the number and variety of changes and reversals in internal reactions and personal behavior required. Each had its own emotional difficulty needing recognition and understanding.

Inner-Directedness and Self-Management

I was amazed during the early days and months of retirement at how much my actions had resulted from forces outside myself since childhood, and how I had become comfortable with this situation. As a child I would ask, "What shall I do next?" and parents were there to tell me. In school there were specific lessons to be learned and rules to be obeyed. (I recall that during one university year I deliberately "cut" classes and spent my time reading in the library. I may have learned as much or more than I would have in classes, but I was severely punished by receiving very poor grades.) At work I had the directions of supervisors to follow. Even with administrative authority there were expectations to be met and others to be satisfied.

Now, in retirement, the supports of childhood and the directions and expectations of the working years were no longer present. There was no one to tell me what to do with my time. There seemed to be no one who cared what I did with my time as long as I didn't trouble others. I, *myself*, had to manage my days. I could be active or inactive, productive or unproductive, growing or stagnating. The decisions were mine. Always decisions. Nothing laid out for me by others. Frightening. There were times when the burden of responsibility to direct and manage my time seemed overwhelming. There were days when I was at loose ends with nothing I really wanted to do. Disliking myself for allowing feelings of passivity and resignation to overcome me, it would take a strong effort to practice golf shots or go on a long walk. Self-direction and self-management, I found, became a heavy price to pay for release from pressure and a drastic change in a pattern of living.

I came to understand why effective self-direction and management was so difficult for many in retirement. Instead of having to make decisions as to how to spend each day, it would be easier to while away the empty hours.

A woman, widowed for a few years and who had had a series of emotional and physical difficulties in adjustment, told me that never before had she faced making decisions. First her parents and then her husband had made the major decisions in her life.

Now she found making even small decisions terrifying. She knew she should be active but she found it easier to sit home with a book and several drinks. She knew she should make efforts to socialize with others, but she found the decision to do so hard to make. It was easier to rationalize that perhaps others might not want to see her. Evenings were both lonesome and frightening. She dreaded arising in the morning to face another empty day.

Hence the change from the direction of one's life from the conditions of work, the directions of others, the constrictions on behavior to conform in order to succeed, the guarding of one's feelings toward others in authority, to a state of self-management and self-direction is one of the most serious and difficult of all the transitions in retirement. It requires awareness of one's self, emotions and strengths to be honest with oneself. Only with such self-awareness can one escape the rationalizations that defeat effective self-management. I write from my own experience.

One man we knew shied away during the working years of his life from looking deeply at himself, his motivations and his behavior. He spoke with certainty about his activities when he retired. He would publish a small-town newspaper. He would find a place remote from people and live off the land. His options, he said, were many.

Then he retired. He attempted none of the projects he had talked about. It was not that he didn't plan for retirement. Rather he had never confronted within himself the rationalizations on which he had built his life. Now he could not admit to himself that his talk had been to enhance his ego. With these blocks to self-understanding, he could not allow himself to find smaller activities lest the image he had tried to build be punctured. He ended a sad and useless man.

This passage into retirement from the partial direction of work conditions and other persons to greater self-directedness gave me much increased self-awareness. I learned much about my reactions to emotional stresses. I learned about my difficulties in relinquishing much that I had striven for, particularly in the area of ego needs fed by rewards and admiration from others. My self-reflection, aided by all the honest discussions with Martha, helped me to seek out the activities that keep me alert but more serene and at peace with myself.

The Disuse of the Wisdom of Age

I discovered another emotional loss problem in retirement to which I needed to make adjustment without bitterness or disparagement. In past generations being elderly supposedly meant having the wisdom and knowledge only years of experience could bring. Youth could respect the elderly and seek some of their wisdom. But the recent explosion of knowledge and the rapidity of technological and social change have made this respect nearly obsolete. The young today rather look to new knowledge not available even a few years ago.

This makes adjustment in retirement more difficult. Not only is one's skill and labor not wanted, but one's knowledge may be almost archaic. It is the elderly who now need to catch up. The rapid growth of adult education courses for the senior citizen is evidence of this point. As I try to find the energy to read even some of the avalanche of professional articles now appearing in my area of specialization and related fields, I recognize my need to keep up with the rapidly changing knowledge and events. I can now recall my own emotional reaction when the first Sputnik crossed through the void. I felt, even then, a sense of personal loss. The guideposts, the certain knowledge I had been taught, were gone. What more would I need to adjust to?

Recently I reread some verses that aptly describe what the knowledge explosion has done to the value of past experience and how the elderly cannot expect the respect of youth.

> The respect of youth
> For the Wisdom of Age
> Decreases as the rate
> Of language evolution
> Increases—
> Because the wisdom of age
> Is couched in the idiom
> Of a world gone by.[1]

Those who retire need to recognize that the working world they left will seldom remember them or call for their continued help. The way to a healthy retirement, then, is to create the conditions where one's abilities and skills can find a new avenue for expression.

Turf or Territoriality

One of my most surprising discoveries in my journey into retirement dealt with what is known in a number of fields as "turf" or "territoriality." Each animal, each plant, each person needs a physical or psychological space that is his. Who has not owned or watched a dog run from another dog in a territory away from home, but who would bark furiously and attack the same dog when around its own home.

In the garden of our home in North Carolina we have a small feeding station for birds. Two mockingbirds rule a space of land some thirty yards on each side of the house. That is their turf or territory. Woe to any bird that violates this space. Occasionally a blue jay will swoop down to grab a piece of food on the wing before being attacked by one of the mockingbirds. Birds may safely roost in trees just outside the zone designated by the mockingbirds, but they may be in trouble if they venture inside the zone.

---

1. Bradford Shank, "Cycle," in *Fragments* (Englewood Cliffs, N.J.: Prentice-Hall, 1959). Used by permission of Mrs. Louise Shank.

Last Spring a tree outside the zone was filled for two days with many cedar waxwings intent on stripping a holly tree inside the zone. We watched the ensuing battle. At first the cedar waxwings flew in large groups toward the holly tree only to be chased away by the mockingbirds. Then they engaged in small forays, seeming to us to be distracting the mockingbirds. Unsuccessful! Finally, after many attempts, they left to find an unprotected holly tree.

We discovered what I suppose each of us had assumed without thinking about in all of our married life, that each had a space, a turf, a territory. For Martha the home had been her nest, her place, her responsibility, her turf, even though she had worked, most often with me, outside the home, and even though somehow I was also part of the home. When we moved about during the early years of our marriage, she planned the actual move and organized the new home. She was the caretaker of the household goods we took with us from place to place. She had only a limited view of my household abilities, undoubtedly sound, and I became more of a helper than a decider in home affairs. The home was her responsibility and her territory.

I had, in turn, my territory. It was the place in which I worked for a major portion of the day. Psychologically it was my position, my role, my responsibility, my status in life to organize and manage. I would return home at the end of the day and hear, perhaps, of some of the events that had occurred there (but not to me), and recount, perhaps, some of the events of my day. It wasn't that we didn't share many events with each other, consult with each other, make many decisions together, or seek help from each other. It was just that Martha had her territory, physically and psychologically, and I had mine. We didn't realize the full significance during those years. It was as simple as that.

Then I retired. I left my turf, my territory, and wasn't wanted there any more. I then intruded on Martha's turf or territory. I realized vaguely that I was intruding, and she began to feel that her freedom was decreased while her workload increased. Spending days at home left me feeling strange and not quite belonging. It was almost like being an alien in a foreign land. We seemed to bump into each other. I seemed to be in the wrong place at the wrong time, and it was not hard to sense her irritation. Escape hatches were few. It was closer living than we had been accustomed to.

I found that if I were to be of help in the home I had new skills and new information to gain. At my age I felt like an inept learner and I know it seemed so to Martha. Now I was a subordinate in another's territory. Before I was the psychological and physical possessor of my territory. This was a drastic change and not one conducive to my self-esteem. I no longer felt the confidence of my professional status. I felt now some of the awkwardness and ineptness of a beginner. It created feelings of hostility toward the total situation of retirement mixed with reactions of self-disapproval.

For me, as a husband, it was an unexpected shock to experience emotionally what leaving one's turf and intruding on another's means and does to one's behavior. The traditonal male role and status of supposedly being the head of the family and its provider no longer has as much meaning as it once did. Authority and status are now questionable. Leaving the turf that gave one self-respect and self-esteem and entering the turf one's wife has possessed for years and has security and confidence in managing, somehow moves a husband from a superior to a subordinate role. A sense of uselessness can be felt. What can a husband add to the competent management a wife has given to the home for many years? Alone time, so necessary for each individual, is lessened. Generally, the least sensitive of husbands recognize the times when their wives wish they were out of the house.

Leaving the situation that gives one identity and a sense of personal value can be traumatic to one's ego. This is especially true when one's turf has provided opportunity to have influence and to be involved in decisions. I realized at retirement that a person whose personal territory was owned and directed by another—who held a job subject to constant orders from someone else in a position which offered no personal satisfaction—must be filled with constant rage at the feeling of worthlessness. Perhaps this helps to explain some of the brutal authoritarian behavior they take on those weaker, such as wife and children, when they come home.

Such a shift in territoriality may have a profoundly shattering and potentially damaging effect on a marriage relationship. The delicate balance of relations built up over the years of marriage has been based on freedom for each partner to have experiences apart, sufficient alone time so each develops an individual identity and a minimum of minor irritations, inevitable when too much time is spent together. Abruptly, with retirement, this delicate balance is disrupted. New relations need to be established. New boundaries set. New patterns of freedom determined.

Martha and I began to appreciate that the shift in our living was far more complex than moving from Washington to North Carolina. We became increasingly aware of the irritations that were building for each of us as more of our time was spent together. We didn't think, at first, of the concept of turf or territoriality. That came later through our discussions. We merely knew we needed to talk about some of the irritations each was feeling and their causes.

We worked first on the roles I could play comfortably in the home—jobs that were mine—so that I wouldn't feel like a flunky taking orders and so I wouldn't be in her way. We took care that her role and responsibility, and her self-esteem as a manager of the home, was not diminished, but at the same time my self-image was not hurt. We worked on ways in which we wouldn't bump into each other. It was clear she considered the kitchen generally off-limits. Long accustomed to being free during the day, I was to get my own lunch if she were not home.

When we had company it was my role to fix the drinks and, if dinner was also to be served, to set the table. My study was my domain, not to be disturbed except by the maid at the weekly cleanup.

We talked about areas of privacy and the importance of doing things with others as well as by ourselves. We both enjoyed golf. Quickly I acquired golfing companions and Martha secured hers. Each would have various highlights and low points in the game on any particular day. This gave something to relate to the other and so on late afternoons whoever had played had a tale to tell of the woes and joys of the day.

As we gained new and deeper understanding of the need for each to have a personal territory, and the intense reactions when restrictions occurred, we began to observe other couples. We were particularly interested in the differing ways husbands reacted to the loss of territory and the ways in which they intruded on their wives. Some husbands over-acted and some under-acted. Those who over-acted tried to regain a turf by dispossessing their wives from theirs. They endeavored to take command of the house and order their wives like servants. Those who under-acted intruded in an entirely different

way. Unable to cope with retirement successfully, they remained unhappy. They stayed at home, expecting or demanding their wives' total time and attention. In both cases, different as they were, the result
was to control their wives and to curtail their freedom.

Being controlled, whatever the method, does much to take away,
or reduce, the sense of personal identity of the individual. More, being controlled by another, means that one has less control over oneself. Losing some measure of control or ownership of one's time and
wishes brings for all who have no need to be dependent on others
submerged or overt hostility or anger. As Martha and I found, even
inadvertent overcrowding of the other creates irritation. To prevent
this we settled on the routine of afternoon tea as a time to review our
problems, give reactions that were helpful to each other, share experiences and make decisions.

It was not only husbands who intruded on their mates' domains,
wives also intruded upon the territory of their husbands or restricted
their previously experienced freedom. Insistence upon greater at-
tendance, or increased time at home, or unusual requests that denied
husbands both alone time and some territory that was their own,
were conscious or unconscious restrictions some wives used. Such
intrusions and restrictions, as we clearly saw, were ways of controlling the other. Being controlled, in turn, creates expressed or unexpressed hostility.

Among the many situations we observed in which the husband's
difficulty with territory affected his wife, the following two illustrate
opposite reactions.

Charles had been a generous man and content with his wife's management of the home. Mary, his wife, had been vibrant and full of energy. Then they retired. His personality and his behavior toward his
wife changed drastically. Leaving his territory and needing another,
he took over the running of the house. He said he could do it more
economically and systematically. When they went shopping and she
would place some product in the basket, he would put it back on the
shelf, explaining that it was too expensive and not necessary. He took
over most of the household responsibilities. He worked out a daily
chart indicating what household activities were to be carried out at
what time, for how long and by whom. He denied her the use of the
car, maintaining that her eyes were less keen than his and her re-

flexes slower, thus making an accident possible. (She had always driven the car without difficulty before.)

She objected, pointing out that she had run the home effectively for many years, but he brushed her argument aside by saying that he had never before had the opportunity to see how a real system could be developed for home-making that would save money—something no woman could understand.

For many years she had submitted to his dominating personality. Now it was a habit. Anger, tears, appeals had no effect. Needing a territory he could control, he had taken hers. She didn't have the strength to fight for her own or to find another. Those who hadn't seen her for some time were shocked at how much she had aged.

One wife told Martha of the smothering existence she experienced since her husband's retirement. She said to Martha, "John has made me his retirement hobby. He is more than a shadow. He has become my alter ego. He goes wherever I go and I seldom have a moment to myself. If I go shopping for clothes, he merely sits in the store until I am finished. I feel tense and unable to shop leisurely. I feel I must hurry over a selection of a dress rather than enjoyably taking my time."

She continued, "Even in the house he wonders where I am if I have gone into another room, and will call me. Sometimes I wait until he is in another room, then hurriedly put on my coat and call to tell him I am hurrying out on a necessary errand. It is my only escape. But when I return home, I find him sitting pathetically in front of the window watching for my return. I can't help but feel guilty and sorry for him, but these feelings are always mixed with anger at the way my life is being controlled."

She ruefully admitted that her guilt, her sorrow for him and her sense of responsibility made it difficult to help him. She had made many suggestions as to things he could do to stay busy, but he always had excuses why the suggestions wouldn't work. Long years of tending for his comfort now made it too difficult for her to tell him with sufficient force what he was doing to her life.

This man was not taking over her territory. He had just moved in on her territory with psychological bag and baggage, expecting her to supply his needs.

Perhaps few couples find a perfect solution to the problem of territory in which the need of each partner is attained without sacrifice upon the part of the other while still making possible sufficient companionship, sharing and communication. For me a patchwork of work, play, leisure, satisfying experiences with Martha gave me back my dignity and identity without interfering with hers. In fact, we were able to discuss openly the needs each of us had, the places where we felt crowded by the other, and the areas we enjoyed sharing, and we found the openness of our communication increased. We discovered we were sharing more private feelings about a multitude of things than we had ever before. It felt good to share feelings, even minor ones, and know the other listened.

All this helped me realize that one of the most difficult and devastating problems to be faced in retirement is the loss of one's territory and the need to find a satisfying replacement. I learned that the loss of territory can bring a lessened sense of self-esteem, failure to find new direction in living, overdependency, goallessness and a feeling of finality to life. The suddenness with which many persons lose their territory or turf creates unexpected emotional upsets. Abruptly there is no call for what one has spent years in doing. Finding a replacement giving dignity and respect as a person requires energy when energy may be low, when enthusiasm may flag and when few opportunities are present. It requires motivation to seek when one is uncertain what to seek, and the acceptance of responsibility to manage one's own life. Made work is not enough and usually leads to further boredom.

Recently I had to take my typewriter to a small town some forty miles away to have it repaired by a special mechanic. The town basically had one major industry, surrounded by the usual number of stores and professional service offices.

The mechanic and I, while he was working on my typewriter, began to talk about retirement. He said he was never going to retire. They would have to carry him out when he died. I asked him why he felt so strongly.

"Take this town," he said. "Most men start working in the mill when they finish high school, or before. They work for the mill for nearly fifty years. Then they are forced to retire. They don't know what to do with their time, so they sit home bothering their wives or go down to the tavern to have a glass of beer. Very few of them live very long."

He continued, "That's not for me. I like what I'm doing and there's not much else I like to do. I couldn't stand just to sit home or spend my time at the tavern. I own this little business. When I get older, I may not be able to work as hard, but there will probably always be some typewriters to fix and I'll keep busy."

I sincerely hope it works out for him because he has made no other preparation. As he talked I thought of our village in North Carolina. In the basement of an old building, a very old cobbler has an ancient shop. I don't know how old he is, but he is far from young. He is a genius in fixing a shoe, no matter how disreputable or badly damaged it is. I am ashamed to pay the small prices he charges—charges better suited to 1910. He opens his shop when he pleases and fixes your shoes at his convenience. He has dignity and a sense of self-worth. He is not waiting to die.

The fact that a surprising number of men die within a year or so of their retirement may have little or nothing to do with the emotional trauma of leaving a long-held territory and with the loss of status and supports for self-esteem. Still this situation merits further study.

Martha and I had long discussions as to whether the single or divorced professional or businesswoman suffered the same difficulties in leaving her turf as did a man. While Martha had worked with me during parts of each year over a quarter of a century, she saw herself basically as a mother, wife, companion and helpmate. Her experiences did not provide an answer.

Did early girlhood experience and training in a home make it easier for her to adjust to the responsibilities of homemaking when she retired?

Do her years of working as a single woman make it necessary for her to maintain an apartment or house and prepare meals for herself, while the working husband had this provided by his wife? Did this not make the turf transition different for the single working woman? After all, there were no new skills to learn, no feeling of being out of place and in someone else's territory.

We asked questions of a number of single and divorced women nearing retirement.

Some said they had disliked the responsibilities of maintaining a home and all of the expectations that went with it. Retirement for them, they feared, meant continuously indulging in conversation about cooking and housework with other women. Dull and to be abhorred.

Others said the greatest disruption would be to no longer enjoy the work or career-related conversation with men and other working women. They saw themselves shunted into the world of elderly widows, seldom included in mixed groups. While working they felt themselves accepted as individuals with others—male and female—engaged in the same work. Now, they feared, they would be seen as "merely" women and not included in serious conversation.

Still others saw that retirement would bring time for special home-related hobbies—cooking, entertaining, as examples.

There were those who said that the experience of working in a man's world gave them further skills and increased confidence so that in retirement they could more readily develop a new career or succeed in important volunteer activities more so than the woman who hadn't worked.

Finally some, desperately fearing retirement, saw only loneliness and loss of present interests before them.

Hence we were left both with a greater awareness of difficulties career women might face, and the realization that the problems of retirement differ among people. There seemed to be no simple or uniform answer to the problems of adjustment to retirement—whether for married men or single women. What did come through was that adjustments were there to be made and the internal strength, self-knowledge and personal pride to prevent failure were the important factors for each individual.

The Changing of Goals

I hadn't thought much about the consequence for me of changing goals. I knew that long-range planning for the organization would no longer be mine. What I hadn't thought about was the change in the distance of goals. Instead of planning for the next ten years, my goals would now, of necessity, be shorter or indefinite in length.

I didn't realize that I faced a sudden, abrupt reversal in my life

*from long-ranged goals to short-ranged goals, and that hidden in
this reversal was the terrible danger of goallessness with its consequent apathy, boredom and depression.*
A feeling of goallessness can creep up on one little by little.
Stealthily. There are days when there seems no purpose in getting up
in the morning because now there is no business to be about. Sometimes it's easier to drift into nostalgic thoughts of the past when one
was strong and energetic or young and beautiful, rather than think of
what one might do in the present. Especially so when the present
seems dark and depressing and the past bathed in a romantic glow.
Without purposes, and goals now more short ranged, it becomes
easy to be inactive. First excuses, then rationalizations until motivation and will weaken. Then one gradually ceases to have pride in
oneself, liking for oneself, belief in one's competence. An individual
can become hooked on goallessness as readily as on alcohol or
drugs. Alcohol and drugs often follow goallessness because they provide a temporary way of blocking out self-dislike.
Retirement brought home clearly to me how purposes and goals
induce and release energy for activities and provide direction
throughout life. To lack purpose is to drift, to be in the doldrums, to
be bored. Funny, also, how goals pass through a cycle from short-
range, "here and now" purposes in childhood, to long-range, "there
and then" purposes through the major middle part of life and back,
at retirement, to short-range, "here and now" purposes. Full circle
has occurred. In childhood, when attention span is short and interest
easily deflected, the questions asked are, "What can I do now? What
should I do next?" And adults give the answer. Gradually, under
societal pressures, goals become long-ranged. Planning for the future contains a "there and then" quality. Abruptly at retirement,
long-range purposes have usually been met and the call is for "here
and now" purposes.
The short-range purposes of childhood and the long-range ones of
the middle portion in life have certain characteristics common to
them but not to the transition from long-range to short-range goals at
retirement. In childhood and youth, adults—parents, teachers,
others—endeavor to supply goals for the young. During the middle
years the organizational requirements and goals plus the need to suc-

ceed in the eyes of others provide goals. But in retirement the individual must suddenly supply goals and purposes. This is a profound difference.

This reversal in both the distance and the motivation for establishment of goals in retirement is far more difficult to cope with than many realize. Certainly I had not thought through the consequences before I retired. After a lifetime of experiencing external circumstances playing a considerable part in one's goals—role expectations, societal pressures, self-image shaped by tradition—it requires considerable insight and will-power to discover, establish, and maintain goals that continue the value of living.

When I first retired I could only think of the inestimable value of not having to be at the office at a certain hour each day. I wouldn't have to rush madly, hoping to catch a taxi to the airport, or sit anxiously while maintenance changes were made in the airplane. There wouldn't be a superfluous number of dull meetings to attend.

It was not too long before this euphoria turned into a form of goallessness. Not only the work purposes of the past were gone, but little in the present carried the same sense of intense purposefulness as did the goals of the past. A morning walk (good for my health), hitting some golf balls to keep in practice, going shopping with Martha (which she may not have enjoyed because her pace of shopping was different from mine), doing whatever came up filled my days. They were dull days without the keen purpose I had known. I wasn't very happy and my discontent was obvious.

Fortunately this period in my retirement didn't last long. Martha clearly, directly, and withholding no punches gave me a penetrating verbal picture of what I was now like, what I was doing to myself, and what I was doing to her. I didn't like what I heard. I didn't like what I saw in my own behavior. I didn't like what I saw in myself. My self-image took a blow. I began not to like myself. But her clear statements awakened me like a morning astringent.

She certainly alerted me to my drifting into goallessness. I could see my discontent quickly leading me into apathy and depression. The stirring-up helped me see how my failure in coping with my reversal in goals was adding to the burden of her own problems of adjustment. This did nothing to enhance my picture of myself as the competent, knowledgeable, supportive, helping husband. I realized then that it was up to me to set challenges, goals and purposes for myself that would keep me an alert and active person.

After Martha's rude awakening of me, I observed more carefully some members of the club who arrived in the morning, sat around drinking coffee and talking about the same subjects each day. One of my friends said, "The purpose of this club is to keep useless persons alive." This, also, made me think about myself. I didn't want to think of myself as useless, and certainly didn't want others to think of me that way.

This reversal in goals was not easy for us to accomplish. But what we did find fulfilling in the "here and now" was our pleasure in sharing present feelings, reactions and thoughts rather than dwelling on what would "happen when." We came to enjoy the beauty around us—the trees, flowers, grass, blue skies and orange sunsets. We observed others. Some, more serene, gained joy from living and from self-rewarding activities they engaged in. Others, more worried, found themselves unable to let go of the past, and spent long hours of turmoil and planning for events not likely to occur for them. The opportunity to take joy from the present escaped them.

One person of our acquaintance with far more financial resources than she could ever need spent her time in constant worry lest she not have enough. In daily contact with her broker in New York in her efforts to gain more money, and with monthly consultations with her lawyer concerning her will, she lived in a dark, shuttered house, made no friends for fear they might seek something of her, denied herself pleasures she could easily afford and lived a disconsolate, lonely life, her gaze focused on a future that would not come for her.

As part of our experience with the reversal of goals, we also discovered, or perhaps rediscovered, the value of routine. We found that routine, if not too demanding nor too exhausting, helped to prevent goallessness. Just as the hours required by the former job gave structure to one's life, so, now, does the routine of certain hours for meals, for afternoon tea, for other mundane affairs in life serve both as a carryover while new goals are found and as a partial structure for living itself.

Routine in retirement should provide certain hours of alone time, for leisure, for new pleasures and new activities. Unlike the routine of the working years which all too frequently prevented time for self-reflection, for relaxing leisure, the routines developed for retirement should be carefully constructed to provide such time and to eliminate undue stress. The routines of retirement are not to organize time for frenetic accomplishment, but rather to organize time to permit opportunity to know and enjoy oneself and to carry out self-rewarding activities at a pace commensurate with one's energy.

As we underwent the travail of changing goals, a number of important points became clear to us.

1. Goallessness is the pathway to discontent, unhappiness, apathy, depression, psychological and physical deterioration. It must be recognized and avoided at all costs if the days of being elderly in retirement are to be vibrant, happy and healthy.
2. Goallessness upon the part of one marital partner creates discontent that spreads blame outward and thus imposes an incredible burden on the other partner.
3. Clinging to past goals merely to cling to the past leads to an inadequate adjustment to the new conditions of retirement.
4. Creating new "here and now" goals, even though past experience may be sometimes used, helps to bring about a successful transition to the phase of being retired.
5. It is not necessary or always desirable that both marital partners choose the same new goals. When it happens it may be beautifully companionable. But when it is forced, discontent and hostility may be felt by the partner accepting the goals of the other. Different goals may give each a sense of personal ownership and achievement to be shared with and respected by the other.

Time

I discovered in retirement a very different relation to time to which my body, my habits and my tension system needed to find adjustment. This adjustment did not occur immediately. Nor, as I observed, did it for others. It took time to free oneself from the internal sense of pressure and frenetic rush to make deadlines and meet appointments. For me there was a short period when I missed the working lunch.

One way in which I realized the slow adjustment to a different sense of time was in my behavior on the golf course. During my working years, when I had a chance to play I always felt rushed—that I could only spare a few hours for the game. If a foursome ahead was slow and delayed our game, I was impatient and anxious to "go through." During the early days of retirement I felt the same way. Only when my companions would say, "What's your hurry? Enjoy the day. You're retired now. Slow up," would I realize that my habits and tension system were still back in my working days.

At first, also, I felt guilty if I was not busy. I had to learn not to feel as if I were driven by outside demands. It took a while to feel comfortable to dawdle over breakfast and hold a leisurely discussion with Martha, something we hadn't done at breakfast for years. Gradually I adjusted to my body clock to fitting my body needs rather than driving myself. I stopped using an alarm clock.

Days melded into each other. Sometimes it was difficult to remember what day it was. Weekends were differentiated by special events that might occur and not by cessation of office work. There were no more blue Mondays.

I recognized suddenly that in a curious way and only to a certain extent I was reacting to a body clock as I had tended to do in childhood. Martha and I recalled that our son, David, when he entered nursery school took nearly fifteen minutes each morning to cross the street to the school. Of course he was always late. Of greater importance to him were all the new experiences to see and marvel about. Then his vision was wide focused so that he saw new leaves on a tree, the sprouting of a flower in our yard, a caterpillar crawling away, water from the previous night's rain running toward a gutter. Where did the gutter lead to? A question that required time to peer into the gutter. He was reacting to his own curiosity and time was regulated by his internal desires. Only gradually did he come to be more controlled by outside clocks.

I observed other newly retired men struggle with the same time problem. Some continued to feel lost without set hours and a long-familiar comfortable routine that regulated their lives. To the discomfiture and confinement of their wives, they demanded set hours for meals. Other activities had their own undeviating time. Body movements showed clearly that to them time was a precious commodity to be fitted into carefully defined slots. In doing so, they failed to realize how precious time is and that it had best be used in retirement in ways that brought happiness, stimulation, new experiences, time for self, and continuing growth.

Others found it easier to learn to relax and become self-directive about the expenditure of their days rather than be controlled by a clock.

As I continued to think about the impact time had on our lives—often a destructive impact—I was reminded of Charles Chaplin's film, *Modern Times*, in which as he learned to speed up the single operation he had to make on the assembly line, he found that in the crowded lunchroom he was using his fork with the same desperate pace he was geared to on the assembly line. No wonder, with modern technology increasing the speed of life, and with communication facilities such that events around the world are known almost instantaneously so that one is constantly bombarded by a sense of a whirling, destructive, agitated society in which no serenity or peace is possible, that people at retirement have difficulty in adjusting to a slower, calmer pace of living. Hence, one of the difficult transitions in retirement is adjustment to time.

The Importance of Friendships

The many losses occurring with retirement—ending of a career, removal of power and authority, changes in purposes and goals, the excitement of new problems, colleagueship, status and self-esteem—all make the continuance and further development of warm human friendships ever more important. Now, if ever, the vital imperativeness of close human contacts is required to prevent loneliness, feelings of deprivation, depression, estrangement and hopelessness. Now the need for close socialization patterns is more sharply focused on such important feeling factors as caring, warmth, sharing, being listened to, enjoyed, accepted. Other factors related to getting ahead, doing business, or having influence belong to the past. In retirement the basic human requirements of having others with whom to share the common experiences of retirement and aging take precedence. All this I experienced sharply.

Old friends take on greater importance because of long-established love and caring. Acquaintances related only to work can be expected to fade away. But of greatest importance, because old friends may not be close by, is the development of new friendships. Not having common work experiences or ulterior motives to bind relationships, new friendships are built on companionship and mutual liking. Because all are aware that these may be the last friendships, concern and caring become uppermost. These friends are the final bulwark against loneliness.

This transition in the socialization pattern, so necessary to ward off many of the emotional and mental ills of aging, is not always easy to make. I certainly found that clinging to past friends alone brought only despair because many were still at work and others geographically distant. Finding and developing compatible friendships requires the willingness to give of oneself and to be open with and sensitive to others.

For twenty-five years my fiends have also been professional colleagues. Friends I had in school had long since disappeared from my life. But these friends of the last quarter of a century were different. We have been friends longer and have endured many struggles together. Many of these friendships have endured. We are glad to see each other when we meet. But I am retired and most of them are not. We now have less in common. Yet their friendship helps to give continuity to my life. Their caring prevents feelings of alienation from my past life.

But this is not enough in retirement. Holding on only to old friends may be a way of denying the new conditions of retirement. In this age, many persons move to another state, another town, or another part of a large city. Any move brings dislocations in daily relations with old friends.

Old friends die or move away and contacts become fewer. Unless new friends and new patterns of socialization are developed, loneliness with all its tragic attributes and consequences can quickly set in. Few situations seem more tragic then the elderly person living without human contacts.

We found, certainly I found, how desperately I needed new friends. Now I needed them rooted directly in shared warmth and human feelings. In our new community were persons retired from a variety of occupations and backgrounds. What one had done before had little significance. What was important was that we were of an age facing the common problem of growing older. No longer did friendship possibly involve the additional values of doing business with each other or of gaining additional position. That time was past. Differences in points of view or in special knowledge were not important. What was needed, certainly I needed, was to like and be

liked, to care for and to be cared about, to share feelings of companionship and human warmth, to enjoy each other as human beings.

All may not feel as I did, but I was happily surprised how many
now sought human companionship based on acceptance of the other
as a person with human feelings. Those I observed who had the
greatest difficulty in finding human companionship were those who
insisted on the recognition of their previous status.

If loneliness is to be avoided in retirement, then finding warm
human contacts becomes of the greatest importance.

The Problem of Power

Retirement taught me a great deal about the importance of power
on the ego, identity and self-esteem of the individual. Perhaps better
said, I saw more clearly the destructive effect of powerlessness on the
emotional well-being of the individual. Based on my own emotional
experiences in retirement, I could now understand the rage, the tendencies and actions to destroy, the despair, the self-loathing and ultimate apathy that those persons have who feel powerless through
much of their lives. Whether the demeaning aspects of their work,
blocks to progress, social stigmas, or subordination in almost every
way to the commands of others, create the feeling of powerlessness,
how can anyone feeling so have any self-respect and dignity?

Everyone needs to be listened to and respected. When this does
not occur the individual feels not only rejected, but depersonalized
and dehumanized. From this situation comes frustration, anger and
the desire to hurt others. If depersonalization continues, apathy and
self-dislike are mixed with buried burning anger. It is often the unnoticed person who resorts to self-destruction or the destruction or hurt
of others. Anything to be noticed and listened to!

Said another way, power provides significance and self-
affirmation. Power is a path to actualizing one's potentials, just as
powerlessness depresses creativity. When one is powerless there is
lack of power to secure power, and the lack of opportunity to express
the felt need for rage leads to apathy, impotence and dulled
acceptance.

Some, by relinquishing dignity and self-respect, utilize powerlessness as a tool for gaining other ends through submission to the more
powerful. I am reminded of a situation I listened to in a training
group concerned with human relations.

Since their marriage, the husband had always purchased his wife's clothes, just as he determined most other aspects of her life. In his need to have power to control, he never considered whether his choice of garments matched her taste. He never realized that he was dehumanizing her. She was a prized possession and a pawn in his rise to greater power. He had rationalizations for his actions. He knew good clothes better than she did. It was important for his position that she dress well.

In the training group for wives she was asked by other women how she felt. Didn't she feel "owned" and overly possessed? Hadn't she lost her own identity? Didn't she feel resistant to his dominating behavior? She answered she knew she didn't have the strength to battle him directly. She had learned that by being submissive she secured more beautiful clothes and more expensive jewelry than she could ever have bought for herself. So she didn't mind. It wasn't worth it to her to try to be her own person.

In my passage through retirement I made the trip from a position (and awareness) of power to a state that approached powerlessness when I experienced various shades of angry and unhappy emotions, and then on to a new sense of power. For many, as well as myself, this must be close to the essence of the problem of retirement. How many stay lost in the web of powerlessness with its terrible cost in feelings of insignificance, loneliness and despair?

When I retired I relinquished much of the power I had spent years in accumulating. I had raised barriers to my opportunity for creativity. I had endangered my sense of significance. Who was I significant to, having experienced the process of being put on the shelf? Looking back at that time, I felt unused and therefore useless. I felt powerless now, where before I had felt power. I felt my abilities were not employed. It was a blow to my self-esteem, with no way that I could see to prove myself and no one to care whether I could. Or so I thought.

Having relinquished power, I needed to find a new and different source of power. This time it had to come from within myself. I had to set up my own challenges of continuing to learn and keeping my mind open and receptive, of seeking new ways of being vibrant and active, of extending myself in communication and contact with others. Only in this way could I maintain respect and liking for myself. By meeting these challenges I was moving from one kind of power, essentially awarded by others, to another kind of power that flowed from me and was a measure of the dignity and strength I wished to maintain for the rest of my life. I needed my own challenges that would enable me to remain strong through the difficulties of aging. Only then could I have self-esteem.

Others who finish this trip successfully obviously do it differently. But they have won out over apathy and the defeat of only "sitting on the shelf." They have found ways of continuing to actualize their potentials, to fulfull their lives, to value themselves, to maintain emotional balance and to enjoy life.

Finding the Proper Pace of Activity

A friend, who was living through his first year of retirement, recently called me. Among the things we talked about was how his retirement was going. He said he couldn't adjust to retirement. Part of him wanted to be relieved of the daily work grind. But another part, and the part he was having trouble with, was a desire to continue using his energy as in the past by working hard. After all, he told me, after nearly forty-five years of working at maximum energy, he found it hard to slow down. Part of him wanted to and part of him didn't. He couldn't find the right balance. He knew he was driving himself more than was good for him physically, but when he tried to ease up, he became edgy and irritable.

I knew what he meant. I had gone through the same process of finding the proper pace of using my energy wisely, but using it. I thought of one of our neighbors who, when he first retired, jogged a couple of miles each day. He purchased a special sweat suit and shoes for jogging. Gradually the time we saw him leave the house and return became shorter. After a while he stopped jogging. At first he told the rest of us how good jogging was and how much energy he had. When he quit jogging he didn't say anything. He continued exercising, like the rest of us, in ways that were more fitted to his energy level and his bodily needs. But he had made the transition from the frantic urge to be in perpetual motion to a wiser use of his energy.

Keeping Fit

Perhaps the major factor, certainly as I experienced it and observed it in others, in living with the aging process is to keep mentally alert and physically fit. Each of these conditions affects the other and the emotional state of the person affects both.

Keeping fit, as the years roll by, becomes increasingly difficult. When I was young, diet and the regularity of exercise was not considered important, or I didn't think about it. Now I am more aware of the importance of good health and the contributions diet and exercise make to it. I pay, the next day, for any major deviation in my diet. Holding to my diet requires more self-control than required in former years. I need a certain amount of physical exercise or my weight increases and ultimately my health declines. There are times when I would prefer to do nothing physical rather than take the required walk or hit a specific number of golf balls. More and more I must be my own careful manager.

A number of examples before me, both positive and negative, help me to maintain a regular regime.

A lovely lady of our acquaintance is now approaching ninety. Two years ago she was mugged on a city street and suffered a broken hip. She is now recovered and each day she walks slowly exactly one mile. Still mentally alert, because she keeps herself that way through conversations with a variety of friends and by serious reading, she plans another book she would like to write. She is well aware of the process of aging and has accepted it as a piece of the fabric of life. But last year she told us, when the question of her age came into the conversation, that she had decided to be sixty-five for the rest of her life.

I think of her on those days when I would like to ignore the challenges I have set for myself. I think also of my father who lived into his eighties. During the Second World War, when he was in his middle seventies, he took pride in doing war work on an assembly line at a nearby factory, a type of work he had never done before. Each day of his weekend he would take a leisurely walk of a couple of miles.

I play golf with individuals with severe physical handicaps, yet who overcome them, and I know persons with less severe handicaps who have given in to them and allowed their health to deteriorate. The reasons in all cases lie inward. One of my golfing companions, now seventy-nine, has two artificial hip joints. His golfing handicap remains a stroke or so below mine, and I can claim no such problem.

Because he says nothing about it, I cannot know what difficulties he must overcome each day he plays, but I do recognize the self-discipline and determination he exerts.

I have learned, since the first year of retirement, how enjoyment in living and happiness with desired activities contribute to keeping fit, both emotionally and physically. Moments of unhappiness or despair, when they occur, create stress and my body tells me the damage stress is doing. Learning to listen to my body and to live within its potentials, seeking emotional reactions that create pleasurable feelings, and accepting the destructive ones of hate and anger and frustration, but not allowing them to remain to fester inside me, become the surest way to make these years of being elderly, but not aged, productive and enjoyable ones. Coming to know myself better and coming to term with what is *me*—both good and not so good—enables me to be more self-directive.

The other day our son who was visiting us said, "Dad, you must be very happy where you are now living and in what you are doing. It shows in your body, your health and your spirit."

While I observed many who overcame many handicaps and lived with dignity, I also observed those who, for a variety of reasons, didn't. There were some who couldn't release the past and so could make no passage into a relaxing and enjoyable retirement. Excessive eating, drinking, smoking were their opiates for unhappiness and their methods of ultimate self-destruction. There were those who could not find the courage to seek new ways to a new life. There were those who waited, unsuccessfully, for others to pull them through the transition period. Finally, there were those whose sense of self-worth was too low to give them confidence that their lives could improve. To me they are engaged in a process of *Gradual Suicide*.

Martha told me about one of her companions. This woman was greatly overweight. Not tall, the weight made her appear very dumpy. On hot days, the heavy, all-enveloping girdle she wore to keep much of the weight from showing must have been torture. One day she told Martha the extent of the dislike she had for herself. She disliked herself for being obese, but her dislike of herself as a person went deeper. It dealt with her perception, that she, an unworthy person, could never exert the discipline to lose weight. It was as simple, and as tragic, as that. Believing herself unworthy, self-discipline was beyond her.

There were others whose dislike of themselves led not only to self-destructive actions or lack of action, but also to the continuous punishment of their spouses for their own sense of inadequacy.

Living with Aging

All of us must ultimately come to terms with the process of aging. I doubt if it is easy for anyone. Some I have known have tried to pretend that for them the process does not exist. Others, to block out the realization, do just the things which hasten aging—excessive drinking or eating, over-expenditure of energy, constant worry and stress.

During my working years, everyone who knew me saw me as a hypochondriac. I burdened my wife and son with inordinate complaints. I panicked at almost every ache or pain, visualizing to myself the direst of consequences. I immediately went to my doctor. Being a caring doctor, he always examined me before reassuring me. I underwent numerous tests to reassure myself.

Not understanding all of my motives, I like to think that during those working years I was obsessed with the fear that I would leave Martha and David without the financial security they should have. This reason sounds plausible and I would like to believe it. I suspect, however, that I took the stress of my work and my anxieties about our many somewhat daring innovations I had introduced into my unique organization out in hypochondria.

Whatever the reasons, retirement brought a change. I worried less about my physical condition, and Martha was aware of much less discussion about my health. I felt, and showed, decreasing concern with the increasing evidence of aging. Perhaps, because many with whom I played golf were older and would say, "Young man, it's your turn to play," I felt younger. Whatever the causes, and undoubtedly the greater happiness I was enjoying had its effect, I learned from experience what I had known before, that happiness and contentment lead to better health.

The answer to living with the acceptance of aging would seem to be:

1. Accept aging as a natural part of the process of life. Really *emotionally* accept it. Don't just speak of it as an abstract fact.
2. Don't use aging as an excuse for rejecting enjoyment in life. Don't give up the benefits of being elderly.
3. Don't give in to the process of aging by neglecting both physical and mental health.

4. Continue to extract from life all that is possible even with physical handicaps.
5. Keep alert and alive mentally. Learning can go on all through life. Keep it up.
6. Be active and productive, even though you are producing for your own happiness and health.

Freedom

I suppose for most persons retirement means freedom. This is probably the way they feel just before retirement. There will be freedom from unwelcome tasks, from early morning rising when one would prefer to sleep, from orders from others, from criticism and competition. But as I found as I struggled with retirement, freedom is a two-edged sword. Certainly, I was free from the load of work and responsibility I had carried for years. But free to do what? What was I to do with all the time freedom gave me? I had to decide each day what I wanted to do, or even what I ought to do. Freedom wasn't always comfortable. It would be easy to sink into doing nothing, sitting around, following Martha on errands. But at what a cost to my own self-respect? Once such a pattern was set, as I had seen in some acquaintances, it became increasingly hard to break. Like dope, the more one took the harder it was to stop. Freedom alone could lead to drifting, drifting to boredom and unhappiness.

It was clear to me that it took strength and resolve to cope with freedom. Freedom meant that I must set my own pattern of goals and activities, and that they should be meaningful, not meaningless, to me and should aid my sense of self-esteem. I saw that I had merely changed bosses. The organization no longer set goals and established tasks for me. I had "bossed" others. Now I faced the harder task of "bossing" myself. Was I strong enough to set my own challenges, my own goals, my own activities and make myself carry them through? I had seen those who didn't seem to have that strength—who caved in at retirement. Retirement didn't give me freedom in the sense of being relieved of responsibility. Retirement rather placed on me the responsibility for motivating myself. Freedom, as it always should, demanded responsibility—responsibility for myself.

Summary

In this odyssey of my adjustment to being retired I discovered not one or two areas of reversal of attitudes but twelve very crucial and unexpected ones I needed to make. A thirteenth, that of the readjustments and renewal in relations Martha and I had with each other, is discussed in the third chapter.

These twelve reversals were laden with emotional reactions with which I had to cope. I had not predicted them. This made their impact all the more startling and difficult to handle. While I suspect all those who retire do not face all of these adjustments, observations of the behavior of others leads me to believe they are common to most.

If each person retiring could have some foreknowledge of their occurrence, coping with these changes might be more successfully accomplished. Certainly they can be considered as danger flags to alert those retiring of possible trouble ahead.

1. Coping with transition.
2. Innerdirectedness and self-management.
3. The disuse of the wisdom of age.
4. Turf or territoriality.
5. The changing of goals.
6. Time.
7. The importance of friendship.
8. The problem of power.
9. Finding the proper pace of activity.
10. Keeping fit.
11. Living with aging.
12. Freedom.

Chapter 2

Martha's Problems

Wives' problems in retirement are seldom considered. Yet wives usually confront difficulties in the same basic areas their husbands do: deep emotional reactions; displacements, disengagements and losses, problems of adjustment through a long transition period. Although the difficulties they face may differ—in fact may be the reverse and reaction to the ones their husbands encounter—they can be extremely acute with severe emotional impact.

In my generation, wives accepted the expectations of what a wife should be like and do, sometimes with resentment at their lot. They know they are expected to follow, solace and care for husbands having problems. As a result, many become victims of the insensitive and demanding behavior of retiring husbands.

This may be why the problems many wives meet in retirement have been so greatly ignored. Books, articles and preparation courses for the retiring husband have been produced in the hundreds, while little has been written or done for the wife retiring with him. After all, so goes the assumption, wives don't retire. They merely continue to manage the home and prepare the meals. Hence, the causes of new irritations, frustrations, anger, disruptions, difficulties with loneliness or the unavoidable process of aging many wives experience have been given little attention. The fears, anxieties and other emotional batterings some wives endure when their husbands retire are disregarded.

Dreading Retirement

I began to have deep fears and forebodings a few years before Leland retired. While he was thinking only of the benefits, I wasn't certain how he would really react to retirement, nor what would happen to me. When he was a little over sixty he talked of retiring before he was sixty-five. My blood seemed to turn to ice. Fortunately, I feel, he waited until he was sixty-five.

My fears came from two sources. Having watched for years the energy and long hours he poured into his work and his dedication to the organization he headed, and having worked with him each summer, I knew very well how challenging, meaningful and enjoyable his work was to him, no matter if he grumbled occasionally about his work. He found it difficult to relax on vacations. On trips abroad he worked incessantly with little time for any sightseeing. What free time was available, he spent talking with foreign colleagues in his field.

With this background I could see no way in which he would not become completely lost when he retired. I was haunted by the specter of a man devoid of new challenges and bemoaning all he had lost. Would I then be left with a desolate, hopeless, unhappy husband hanging around the house and making my life miserable with his complaints? No wonder I had forebodings.

The second source of my fear concerned myself and my own life at retirement. The thought of twenty-four hours a day spent with Leland, or anyone for that matter, presented a picture of complete disaster. I appreciated my privacy and freedom during the day. Would I be forced in retirement to give these up to satisfy his desires?

When we retired what new interests and activities would be available to me? This question disturbed me, but, unfortunately, not enough. Almost all of my foreboding grew out of concern for what his retirement would do to him and to me, and not what retirement would do to me. I learned later how unbalanced my fears were.

Because of my fears, during the few years before Leland retired, I talked to a considerable number of women I knew whose husbands were in their middle years or older. Most had the same concerns I did.

One woman told me, "I know I'll go crazy with Joe around the house all day when he retires. I don't think I'll be able to take it."

A divorcee told me, rather dramatically, "If I were still married and had to retire with him, I think I would have to kill him."

Another wife, with children grown and away from home, said, "I can't conceive of retiring with Bob. Now he comes home from the office, has a couple of drinks, eats his dinner, often in silence, watches TV until bedtime, then goes to sleep. What, in Heaven's name, will retirement be like?"

A wife who worked told me, "I'm going to continue working until I drop. Twenty-four hours a day with my husband would drive me up the wall."

One wife reminded me of experiences I had had. She said, "When Jim and I used to go out to dinner alone, we generally had little to say to each other. Silence existed while we ate. I used to look around the restaurant and sort out, in my own mind, which couples in the room were married and which were not by the animation of the conversation and the attention shown toward each other. I used to wonder what we would have to talk about when Jim retired. The future didn't look bright to me then. It turned out better than I expected, although our communication could be better."

Still another wife told me, "I'm really looking forward to having all of my husband's time and attention when he retires." I thought she must be dreaming.

Dislodgment from Home and Disengagement from Family and Friends

One of the most devastating emotional problems many wives face lies in moving from the home in which she has lived—her nest—for many years and moving somewhere else. At the time there may be sadness at the breaking up of a home and some hostility toward the new owners because they will change aspects of the house most dear to her. For the wife leaving the home, even if it is to go to an apartment in another part of the city because a big house is too much for two people, the break is somewhat similar to the disengagement and loss the husband feels in leaving work in which he has spent much of his life. For both the shock and the deep emotional reactions will be felt later and for some time. For the wife, not only is there the dislodgment from the home but the disengagement of close and often daily contacts with family, friends and neighbors. Again, this dis-

engagement for the wife is not unlike the loss of work companion-
ships her husband feels. Routines for both are broken. New ones
must be established and new contacts made. The losses are made
more difficult because each feels the individual loss is unique and
not fully understood by the other.

Certainly I found all this true for myself.

I had sworn to myself that I wasn't going to be like my mother. I
wasn't going to tamely follow Leland's decisions and hide my feelings. I wasn't going to say yes when I meant no. We did have a long
discussion as to where to go when he retired. I remember saying
flatly that North Carolina was as far south as I would go, but it turned
out that North Carolina was exactly where he wanted to go. What I
did hide from him was my realization that I wasn't ready to leave
Washington. I guess I went along with the move out of Washington
because of my acceptance of the wife's role, his strong desire to leave
the city where his organization was located, and my concern about
how unhappy I thought he would be in the city without his work.

As we made the move I recalled again my mother's life. For a few
years, when I was a child, we lived in Florida. My mother hated every
moment of the time—the heat during the summer, the flatness of the
land, the insects—everything. Then we moved back north. After all
the children left home, my father insisted on retiring to Florida and
my mother went with him. I was surprised she would go, remembering how much she complained when we lived there.

After they retired I visited them. I vividly recall my mother meeting me at the train station and telling me immediately how much she
hated moving to Florida. I knew she wouldn't say anything to my father and I could sense how unhappy she was with retirement. I
vowed then that I was not going to do the same thing myself, but I
did.

I think, although I'm not certain, that the home means more to
most wives then to most husbands. Certainly it means something different. The home is the wife's place, her responsibility, the area in
which most of her time is spent. The husband normally has a different place where he works each day. He comes back to the home at
night and during weekends.

In our case there was no doubt of the difference. For Leland, because he traveled so much around the country and to various parts of

the world, Washington was a place from which he went and to which he returned. For me our hundred-year-old Georgetown house was my precious nest and Washington a city I loved so much I felt I could never get enough of relishing all its sections. I particularly loved the tree-shaded streets and cobbled sidewalks of Georgetown. Even after the many years of living there I could sense, each time I went out, the long history of the place, and I felt I was a part of it.

When we did sell our home and move, I felt dispossessed from the home and city in which I had spent more years of my life than anywhere else. At first sadness and then hostility built up in me. I not only felt hostile toward Leland but also toward myself. I remembered that in some of the groups I had been in, the following points were heavily stressed. They certainly related to me now.

1. Healthy persons should be sufficiently assertive to maintain their own identity, but many wives because of role expectations tend to bury their own feelings to agree with their husbands. *(That had been me!)*
2. Healthy people should be their own persons, but many wives give in to their husbands' wishes. *(I had given up what I most wanted to please Leland and had said nothing about my feelings. I had said yes when my inner desires dictated no.)*
3. A person's greatest task is to gain psychological interdependence, but wives are expected to be dependent. *(After all my training and Leland's help toward making me consider myself, as an individual, I had worried sufficiently about him that I agreed to our move.)*

During the year after we moved I talked to various other "retired" wives. Some found leaving the place where they had always lived a separation bringing quite deep emotional reactions. Others found the disengagement from long-held friends and neighbors most difficult. They said it was hard to replace such relationships quickly. Still others had been doing volunteer work or holding organizational positions they hated to leave. They felt they had been forced to break up happy patterns of living against their own desires. However, as I realized much later, none of the wives compared her losses and sense of forced change with the similarity of her husband's losses in different areas. This lack of communication of real feelings between wife and husband, I saw, led to each feeling sorry for himself and not very aware of how the other partner was feeling. Certainly this seemed true of wives who tended to hide their feelings and express them only to other wives.

For me, leaving Washington was a matter of timing. Though I knew the move was approaching, I was not ready for it even though Leland certainly was. A year or so later, after I had made numerous trips back and found how changed everything was and how friends had left, I became comfortable in North Carolina. I discovered another wife who went through the same experience I had, which was reassuring.

This woman had not wanted to leave Boston, which she loved as much as I did Washington, and move to North Carolina. She knew, however, how intensely her husband wished to come so she agreed without saying how she really felt. But after she lived here she realized how greatly she missed not living in Boston. Her husband wisely suggested that she return to Boston on trips as often as she wished. After a year of making frequent trips, she found her interest in Boston dwindling as old friends moved away and new events of which she was not a part took place. She realized then that you really can't go back again, and that new friends and new activities must be found.

Another story I was told described the difficulties a wife faces in moving from a long-established residence when her husband retires. In this case the husband tried to make the separation more palatable to his wife through what amounted to a bribe. As a family they had lived, and raised children, in an apartment in the city. During these forty-odd years the wife had dreamt of a home of her own instead of a rented apartment. Her husband promised that if she would move south when he retired, he would buy a house and she could furnish it as lavishly as she desired. She was delighted. But even with this dream made reality, her first year in the new home was not a happy one. She felt uprooted and in a strange and unfamiliar environment. She missed her church work, her friends, her established daily routine in the city.

I didn't realize the profound influence my decision to leave Washington and move with Leland to North Carolina would have on my emotions and behavior. The repercussions were certainly as acute as any he felt in the turmoil of his retirement.

Our new home in North Carolina was beautiful but I could generate little interest in decorating and arranging it, so we employed an interior decorator. I was urged to join the women's club within the larger country club, a quite select group not ordinarily easy to join. The details of my election were arranged but I was sufficiently indifferent that I hardly knew and didn't appreciate the efforts made for me.

During the first year I knew I wasn't myself. I was unpleasant to others at the slightest provocation. It wasn't clear what was happening to me, but I didn't like my behavior and I wasn't happy about myself. Yet I couldn't stop. It was I, not Leland, who developed all kinds of aches and pains. He had been the hypochondriac while I always had to be dragged to the doctor. Now the situation was reversed. I would complain each morning about my insomnia, my headaches, my other symptoms. I spent a week in the hospital for a thorough check-up, but nothing physical showed up. I just missed Washington and all of the events there dreadfully.

During this year Leland was having his own problems of adjustment to retirement. He would work hard in his consulting work to prove to himself that he had not lost any ability and then complain because he wasn't happy doing it. He would tell me all about his feelings of being unwanted and neglected by former colleagues.

His complaints hit me hardest when I was reaching the bottom of the valley of my own despair. That was when I blew up, telling him how I felt about being taken away from Washington to suit his desires. Fortunately he could listen, try to understand and try to talk problems through without fighting or recriminations.

I could see that my uncontrolled snapping at even the smallest event, Leland's complaints and preoccupation with his problems and my attempt to deny my hostility was breaking our sharing and communication. As we talked, we both recognized that his driving himself in the consultation he now disliked, his complaining, my irritability, illness and final blow-up were all acts of violence directed at each other and ourselves. We realized that neither of us had expected to have as deep emotional reactions to the adjustment to retirement as we did. We both agreed that we had to work together in facing our problems rather than each becoming a victim of emotions that were harmful to ourselves and to each other. As each of us wallowed in self-pity, neither recognized how much more difficult it was for the other.

One decision came out of this first discussion. I should make as many visits back to Washington as I wished without feeling guilty about leaving him alone. He, in turn, didn't have to feel guilty because he didn't accompany me each time. We had taken the first step toward recognizing and dealing with some of the unexpected emotional reactions we each had, and in working out a relationship giving each of us freedom. We did this in a way that strengthened, rather than strained our relations with each other.

Territoriality and Intrusion of Husband in Home

What many wives fear—certainly I did—was having a husband home all day, interfering in various ways with his wife's life. As I talked with newly retired wives and wives whose husbands were about to retire, I received confirmation of the extent to which many wives suffer this worry, anxiety or fear. Most wives told me they didn't want to stir up an argument or be accused of nagging. Many, furthermore, were aware that their husbands were going through a very difficult adjustment.

The various stories told me, as wife to wife, led me to think of, and then compose a hypothetical letter that a hypothetical wife might have written to her husband. The letter would give her husband a chance to learn of her feelings while alone, thus preventing the bitter argument if she had related her reactions verbally.

Here is the hypothetical letter I wrote as a result of the stories I heard. I suspect parts of it will ring true for many wives.

Dear Fred:

After nearly forty years of our marriage I thought I knew you and could predict your moods and actions. But in the six months since you retired, I've felt I've been living with a stranger—a stranger who has been messing up my life and driving me up the wall. Sometimes I don't recognize the man I've lived with and I wonder if you would recognize yourself.

I know you don't mean to make my life miserable—but you do. I suspect you're not aware of how much you have changed and I don't think you would like the picture of yourself you are showing.

During all the years of our marriage I planned and prepared all our meals with careful thought to a balanced diet and nutritional quality. Over the years I've built up a card file of excellent recipes which I periodically review in terms of our dietary needs. I planned weekly menus to give us variety without neglecting nutritional needs. You probably didn't know that any more than I knew many facts about your work.

You never complained about any meal I prepared. In fact, from time to time you would say how satisfying a certain meal was.

No more!

Now you sit in the large over-stuffed chair in the living-room (I wonder if that chair hasn't taken the place for you of the executive chair you had in your office) and tell me exactly what each meal should be. How come? Why have you suddenly decided that you know more about planning meals than I do? It has been one of my jobs for much of my life.

How do you think I feel? I'll tell you. I feel like a short-order cook in a cheap restaurant, and I don't like it.

Another thing. I appreciate your willingness to accompany me when I go shopping. I know you want to be helpful. But I don't appreciate your telling me what I can purchase and what I can't. I'm not incompetent. I'm not yet senile. So why? For years I've carefully planned my shopping, looking for sales and savings without sacrificing quality. I know about labels.

I've saved us money over the years by careful shopping. Aren't you even a little bit sensitive to how angry I feel when you dictate what I should purchase? Are you confusing me with one of your lowest level file clerks in the organization you left?

My dear, do you know you've become quite irascible since you've retired? You're like an angry bear. We used to be able to discuss subjects calmly and share thoughts. No longer. Your opinions seem set in cement and you get angry, and may I say timidly, a little patronizing if I disagree with you. I overheard you sounding off to John the other day as if you were the final authority. You didn't convince him. All you did was make him wary of any future discussion with you. That's pretty much the box you've put me in. I feel I must pacify you, like a child, but you're too old for that.

Have you forgotten that you promised to share some of the household work with me, now that you have time? You were going to empty the garbage and waste baskets each day. You did—for about a week. Now I must put them in front of the door so you have to empty them or stumble over them.

One more thing. When my women friends come for bridge during the afternoon, you really don't need to hang around. They're not half as glad to see you as you think. You put a damper on "women's talk," which is part of our pleasure in playing bridge. You would be annoyed if I interfered with your time with other men. It works both ways.

Finally, my sweet, I've retired too. Remember? I have my own problems of adjusting to a new life. I don't need yours in addition.

I know you are having a difficult time in handling your retirement, but you really are going to have to shape up and solve your problems. At present you are playing havoc with my life and I need a little peace. Please try.

Your loving wife

This letter sums up a wealth of stories told me by retired wives.

Their turf, their territory had been invaded with a host of different consequences. Some wives endured as best they could the continuing complaining of ego-deflated, previously active men who now, not knowing what to do with themselves, turned to their wives for help and companionship.

One woman said, "It's more disruptive and confining than having a baby. At least a baby sleeps much of the day."

A very different complaint was voiced by some wives. They said having their husbands home merely increased their workload. Rooms would be strewn with newspapers, chairs misplaced, ashtrays overflowing.

Some wives mentioned another problem, one that I suffered and never seemed to solve or learn to keep away from. The situation always brought my exasperation to the boiling point. The script always went something like this:

I would be upstairs needing an old towel for cleaning. I would call downstairs to Leland and say: "Please look in the lower cabinet next to the refrigerator and bring me an old towel you will find there."

A voice would float up the stairs, "Do you mean the upper or lower cabinet?"

My heart would sink because I knew what would happen. I would curse myself for falling into the same trap again.

"The lower one," I would shout down.

There would be a prolonged silence, with some rattling of pans and I knew he had first chosen the wrong cabinet. Then all would be quiet for a moment while I wondered why I hadn't gone to get the towel in the first place.

Then I would hear a voice again. He would call, "It isn't here."

Trying to swallow my irritation, I would drop what I was doing and go downstairs to the kitchen. There, on the right-hand edge of the lower shelf in the lower cabinet next to the refrigerator would be a small stack of old towels and cloths I used for cleaning.

He would say, "Why on earth would you put them there?"

In calmer moments I would wonder why I expected him to be successful. He had neither the training nor aptitude for doing things in the house. When I was in the kitchen hurrying to get things ready, he would come in and try to be helpful, but he succeeded only in getting in my way and arousing my frustration and impatience. It always

seemed he stood exactly where I was going to move. I remembered
what a carpenter had told me when we were building a house. He
said that two carpenters couldn't work out of the same tool box.

It was clear, as we discussed it, that each of us was reacting in different ways to the turf problem—he to the loss of his and I to the intrusion on mine. It meant that we needed to work out arrangements
that didn't permit the problem to create emotional tension and disturb our relationship.

Curtailment of Freedom

The problem mentioned by almost all wives dealt with the curtail-
ment of their liberty and freedom of movement and time. Husbands
home much of the time made their wives almost subject to call and
interrupted long periods in the day when they could do many of the
personal things they wished to do. While the wives didn't confront
the sudden, shocking ending of a work career or the change from being active and involved to the stage of having nothing to do that their
husbands faced, now they encountered almost the reverse.

Previously they had had most of the day to themselves. They could
engage in social or volunteer activity but at least they were doing
what they wanted to do. Now they felt they were often at the beck and
call of their husbands. If a husband wanted to go some place, they
felt obligated to go along. Even if not obligated, they would feel sadness and guilt at seeing their husbands go off alone, desiring their
company. If filling his time meant doing it with his wife, she felt she
should do it with him. Not knowing when he would be home or
come home if he went out, many a wife found it difficult to plan her
day. A number of wives said they felt a continuing sense of tension,
whereas before they had felt more relaxed during the day.

A large number of wives implied or admitted a feeling of hostility,
even anger at times, that their husbands expected this attention from
them and never considered that they, the wives, had their own problems, of adjusting to their husbands' retirement. They felt particularly put-upon, because they felt their husbands never considered how
they would feel if their time and plans were continually interrupted.
So this assumption that wives were merely to be present when
needed, and the lack of awareness of their feeling was, I heard again
and again, most galling. Many felt they couldn't talk about it with

their husbands without precipitating a quarrel or hurting their husbands who were already suffering the pangs of separation from their work.

Hence the emotional reactions many wives endure were the opposite of those felt by their husbands and were, to a large extent, caused by the problems husbands encountered.

Lack of Communication

Some wives talked to me about how little their husbands and they had to talk about. They admitted that before retirement they hadn't talked much either, but then there were separate tasks and responsibilities and less time. They had thought that with more time together and less pressing obligations, there would be more time for conversation. Now there was a death-like pall when they were together. Little was said or communicated. A few wives told me they made it a point to think up things to talk about to eliminate the horrible silence that usually prevailed. The trouble, they said, was that their husbands responded with grunts or monosyllabic reactions. What this did was to inhibit them from sharing pleasurable experiences or feelings. The longest period of talk usually came during a quarrel. Fortunately for me the many years of experience Leland and I had had in conducting or being in training groups concerned with human relations had helped us in communicating with each other.

Lack of Understanding between Marital Partners

In my conversations with other wives I became increasingly aware of how each partner grew less understanding of changes in the other. More and more each assumed the other was the same as in years gone by. The rush of events, the separate existences each lived during much of the day, the familiarity that marriage produces all tend to prevent the sharing of personal, intimate feelings giving each more knowledge of the other.

Quite a few wives told me they found it difficult to tell their husbands little experiences they had had or pleasurable feelings they have. They felt that as a result a major part of their personality was unknown to their husbands.

Leland told me of an experience he had on the golf course. He talked to one of the foursome, a new arrival in the community. He hadn't played with him before. Leland had asked the man if his wife played golf. The response was that she didn't but she had plenty to keep her occupied. Leland asked, "Isn't she lonely? What does she find to do in this place where everyone plays golf?" "I don't know," was the reply, "but I'm sure she finds things to occupy her."

Another story illustrates the same theme. In a recent television picture, a well-dressed man living in a beautiful home turned to his shocked wife as he was being led away by the police for a series of crimes he had committed and said, "Remember me as you thought I was."

The inability to share and communicate precious personal feelings with someone with whom one has lived closely for many years creates an inner loneliness somehow different, it seems to me, than the loneliness a woman, or anyone, feels who has no one to talk to even about incidental things. This is loneliness in the middle of a supposed companionship. For me, the inability to tell Leland funny experiences I have had or to discuss serious issues because he might not listen attentively, or fail to understand and respond to me, or would ridicule or tell me not to feel as I do, would wall me off and drive me inward until I would feel I was living two lives with him— the part I disclosed and the larger part I kept hidden.

It seemed so important to me that we have open and free sharing—as it fortunately was important for him also—that our retirement should increase our understanding of the feelings and needs of each other.

I've often thought how wonderful it would be if wives and husbands could briefly switch sexes and roles to know how the other felt. If husbands, for example, could have a short experience with the joys, exasperations and feelings of being vitally needed that are a part of motherhood, and then feel the pangs of loss as children go off to school and away from home, if husbands could experience, even momentarily, the subtle and not so subtle ways in which social pressures and role expectations combine to make many wives of my generation feel inadequate and dependent on men, then communication between wives and husbands might increase and be more understanding. If wives, on the other hand, could experience many of the competitive problems and ego blows most men face, they could better understand the difficulties men face in retirement.

I still remember a humorous book I read many years ago. I think the book was written by Thorne Smith and was entitled *Turnabout*. In the story, a husband and wife are having difficulty in understanding how the other feels with consequent arguments and quarrels. Unbeknownst to them, a little god was perched on their mantelpiece, as I recall the story. The god decided to do something about the situation and so, for a time, he put the husband in the wife's body and her in his body. The laughable situations that followed, of course, made up the book. While I don't advocate little gods on every couple's mantelpiece, I have come to know how much effective communication depends on being *really* able to understand how the other partner is feeling.

Loneliness

I found a number of wives who were lonely and depressed. They had not been able to make the adjustment to a new place to live, a new pattern of living, another circle of friends and intimates. Particularly, they hadn't adjusted to the problems an equally depressed husband was facing in retirement.

In previous days these women often had found little to do except care for the home. They had been dependent on the small circle of friends and intimates they had enjoyed for many years. They had allowed themselves to fall into a comfortable rut, living in the same place for years. Their days were laid out for them with the same home responsibilities. The small circle of friends met almost daily or held long telephone conversations with each other. Over the years they talked about the same things, their homes, husbands, other women. Afternoon television programs and gossip magazines were the source of what information came their way. They did not change their pattern of behavior or grow intellectually over many years. They were comfortably walled-off from the changing world.

When they were rudely yanked out of their comfortable rut at the retirement of their husbands and moved to a new place, they confronted the almost impossible task of being active and developing new friends. They lacked the initiative to make friends and were fearful that they might not be accepted.

One retired friend, widowed but very active, wrote me. She said, "This place where I now live has a lot of 'Clinging Vines' who lean on everyone in sight and who seem to have no inner resources. They have only learned to be dependent on others, not just for material things, but for psychic satisfaction and a sense of meaning."

Many wives retire two to three times during their lives. So their retirement with their husbands differ sharply from the husbands. The wife's retirement is periodic, not sharp and sudden as is her husband's. Therein lies a great difference and the root of many misunderstandings between husband and wife. When the last child trudges off to school, some responsibility is lessened, and a type of retirement occurs. When the last child leaves home for college or to marry, and the house seems empty, this time is the mother's second retirement. The third occurs when the husband retires and reenters the home. Maybe this is reverse retirement.

My Previous Disengagements

During those few years before retirement, while I had those anxieties about Leland in retirement and the possible dreadful consequences for me, as well as feeling the fear and hostility at the adjustments I would have to make, I also thought about our different experiences in "being retired." I had been partially retired twice. He never. At the time I thought his lack of experience in retirement would have serious consequences when we retired. I, with previous experiences of adjusting to losses in responsibility, should be able to cope easily with just another one. He, with no such previous experience, should find coping almost impossible. Or so I thought. And so I worried.

During the six years between the birth of our son and his entrance into school, my life was almost entirely confined to home and child. There was extra housework and hours to be spent with an emerging personality. Even though the end of the day would find me exhausted, I felt the joy and thrill of being needed. David's very existence as well as the direction of his development depended upon my love and care and attention. Bringing up a child from the first moment of infancy is an all-absorbing portion of life for all mothers who want and love children. A child is so very dependent in the early years. I think that all mothers who care, as I did, find these years excessively wearing and absorbing, but providing a feeling of being needed and wanted, and of fulfilling themselves. I suppose few husbands, with their attention also focused on their work, can know the pleasure and enjoyment motherhood brings.

Then came a time when David trudged off to school to return later in the afternoon. I felt both relief and loss. The freedom of those few hours was good for me. I could relax—something I realized I needed. For a little while it was my lazy time. However, I felt a sense of loss during my sudden aloneness. But I saw that I was still needed, although in a slightly different way. David would tell me of his adventures in the new world bounded by the school—what he had learned, his feelings about his teacher, his peer relationships, the trouble spots in his adjustment for which he needed both comfort and counseling. Although his world was expanding, it was extremely clear how much I was needed by him for stability and security, for love and comforting, for correction and direction.

I became very aware that this was a turning point, not only in David's life, but very greatly in mine. His adjustment in school was normal as was the diminishing of his dependency needs on me. I knew that this was how it should be.

But I could not help feeling a mixture of emotions at his first real disengagement from dependence upon me and the reduction of responsibility in my life—pleasure in my newfound freedom, happiness in David's growth as a person, loneliness and a sense of loss about being less needed and some guilt at feeling thus. I didn't think Leland could have fully understood my ambivalence. He was busy assuming more responsibility at work and driving harder. I suppose he felt glad that I had some relief and time to myself, and happiness at David's process of growing up.

After a bit I realized that I must find constructive and growthful activities to fill these alone hours. It would be so easy to drift and grow stale. One event helped me realize that six years had slipped by—years that had been so absorbing that I had given little thought to affairs outside the home. The boundaries of my life had been the home. The event occurred shortly after David started in school. Some educational conference was being held in Washington, where we were then living, and Leland brought a number of persons home one evening, both men and women, to discuss a problem that was to be brought up in the conference the next day. I listened to the conversation but it had an unfamiliar ring to it. I felt very much out of the discussion and consequently insecure. I realized then how much those six years had not only been fulfilling in one way, but now represented another kind of loss and danger to me. I could not let those hours of freedom while David was in school be frittered away while Leland and David continued to grow.

Years later, when Leland was talking about his retirement, I recalled that evening and how it helped me to handle constructively the emotional problems of that partial retirement. Knowing that Leland had never experienced such a situation increased my worry about his retirement. I was tempted to tell him the story but I didn't think it would penetrate his unshakeable belief that he would find the transition to retirement easy to make.

After this evening, I deliberately made more friends, attended events during the day in Washington, visited the Senate and the House and went to committee hearings open to the public. I visited and revisited the various museums, art galleries and exhibitions that make Washington so famous. I remember suggesting to Leland that he take some time off and visit one of the museums with me, but he responded by saying he had seen it before. I realized that I must be personally responsible to keep myself growing and also, if and as opportunity permitted, to keep abreast of his work so that our communication could be as open as possible.

Fortunately, a few years before David entered high school, Leland helped start, and then directed, the training laboratories in Maine. Each summer as a family we went to Maine and I quickly became involved in many aspects of the laboratory and in many of the training groups that were held. I attended many of these unique training groups bringing greatly increased understanding of myself, my reactions, feelings and motives, and certainly increased sensitivity to others. Later I worked with some wives and teen-age groups. At the same time, because I was responsible for housing of participant families in the small town, I came to know practically everyone, locals and participants. This experience was to have tremendous importance to us as a couple, particularly after we retired, but that becomes another part of this story.

The point of importance is that I had had a deep emotional experience of disengagement, of being less needed, of suddenly feeling partially dispensable. Leland was not to have this experience until he retired. No wonder I worried. Would he be able to accept the losses he would suffer and build a new life for himself as I had had to do?

David's high school years, while still part of this first disengagement, lessened my feeling of being needed by him even more. I could widen my scope of interests and at the same time develop a new kind of relationship with him. He was old enough so that we could have adult interests in common. Leland had to travel very much during those years, and while he was away David and I would go out to dinner, to plays, movies, symphonies. One year Leland's work took him to Europe for several months and David and I accompanied him. While Leland conducted group sessions or visited adult education programs (a second career he was then engaged in while he was building the training laboratory) in a number of countries, David and I spent our time in seeing new places and experiencing different cultures. Not only was it good for my growth but it was fabulous to watch a sixteen-year-old boy visibly expand.

The Second Semi-Retired Experience

When David went away to college, I suffered another tremendous loss. I remember vividly driving him to Oberlin on a September day. When we stopped in front of his dormitory, he hurriedly opened the door, grabbed his two suitcases, and rushed into the dormitory. It was very clear that mothers were not only not needed but not wanted when a boy entered college. It was a sad, lonely drive back to Washington.

For a long while I felt a dreadful void. No longer in the late afternoon would I hear the front door slam and a cheery voice have something to tell me. This loss was greater than when David entered first grade. I found myself setting three places for dinner. The few hours between the time when David would return from high school and Leland from work now seemed interminable. Our large house felt terribly empty. The silence was like a heavy blanket hanging over the home.

This was retirement with a vengeance. While my care and concern for David would always remain, I realized that my basic task as a mother was largely ended, even though the obligations of maintaining a home and being a wife remained.

I had a great need to discuss my feelings with Leland, knowing that he would listen and try to understand. I realized that he couldn't feel the way I did. His work was becoming more and more absorbing and time consuming, whereas mine was going in the opposite direction. He did suggest that I go on more trips with him, but most of his trips were short hops from one city to another and this didn't sound like a good antidote to my feelings of loss.

I felt disposable and I almost slipped into a state of boredom and depression. It was hard to find much good about myself. At this stage it would have been easy to have drifted into a useless woman's life of occasional luncheons with other women in the same fix, eased by a couple of martinis, and complaints to Leland about my useless life.

Fortunately I happened to have a conversation with a woman I knew whose youngest daughter had also just left for college. She said her life for many years had been totally occupied with a number of children, home and husband. She, too, felt the loneliness now. She tried to get her husband to understand how she felt, but he brushed her off by saying, "What are you complaining about? You've done your job in raising a family. Relax and enjoy yourself."

In other words, "You're through. You're retired. There's not much more for you to do."

Her talk helped me. I resolved that I was not going to be and feel useless. Again I busied myself as I had done before in taking advantage of the many events in Washington. I volunteered to spend part of each week at Junior Village where children lived who were without a mother's care for a number of reasons, and who desperately needed love and attention. It was a wise decision because once again I felt needed and useful. I met other women facing similar problems and we joined forces in devoting time to a needed cause, while helping ourselves. My circle of friendships grew. Then there were the summers in Maine when I became more deeply involved in the laboratory and I could work with Leland. I became a needed fixture in the summer community. It was a great time for my personal growth and learning.

Increasingly during the winter Leland conducted programs in other parts of the country. There were more groups I could attend and there was more for me to learn. This learning increased my understanding of myself and my relationships with others. It made communication with Leland more direct and open. I was building a life for myself that increased my self-respect and fulfillment.

This second retirement better prepared me, I thought, for any problems retirement might bring. I worried more about Leland because he hadn't had these experiences. I felt secure in my ability to adjust to this new phase of our lives together. How wrong I was.

Retirement

When we retired and moved to North Carolina—it wouldn't have mattered much where we moved—each of us ran into a number of unexpected emotional problems, as we both have discussed. It took much talking together to work our way out of them.

Fortunately our years of working together in the areas of sensitivity and communication made it possible, after a few starts, for us to talk together. It took many weeks and months of leveling with each other, of being honest in expressing our feelings, for both of us to make the long ascents from the desolation we were in. We helped each other. Neither pulled the other up. We pulled ourselves up together and learned much in the process.

Our talks became increasingly open, honest, revealing of our full feelings. As we shared our problems we were able to explore them more deeply and thoroughly. We became clearer about the traps we laid for ourselves and we recognized more and more of the areas of adjustment created by our retirement. Our talks led us to try new activities and to make certain changes in our attitudes and relationships with each other. This provided rich food for discussion and led into further activities.

Luckily the friendliness and hospitality of the people we met softened the transition for us and alleviated some of the strangeness of the move to the new area.

As a result of our discussions I took various steps. First, I generated conversations with other women I knew. I was surprised by the amount of unhappiness and loneliness I found among the wives I talked to. Of course there were exceptions. Many wives said they were very happy in retirement. It became clear that in these cases both husbands and wives had separate cherished activities that involved them individually. Each partner was happy. Neither monopolized the other and neither was without rewarding activities. But in the situations where wives were not happy, none felt she could talk her problems over with her husband nor could she express her feelings without seeming to be a complainer.

Most of these wives said they faced their husbands' expectation that they would follow them without complaint. As a result they smothered their emotions and lived with the belief that their problems would not be heard.

The second step I took was to endeavor to turn my negative attitude into a positive one by seeking out activities. I started to play more golf and I found that as I approached the game more positively I both played better and enjoyed it more. I made more acquaintances and I discovered that most of the women I played with didn't take the game too seriously. We could all laugh, including the victim, at a dubbed shot. Sometimes our play became hilarious. Golf was the excuse that brought us together for companionship. Between shots we would have fun chatting. There was always the pleasure in a good shot and I found golf far more enjoyable. I would come home physically tired but pleasantly relaxed and tell Leland some of the laughable experiences of the day.

One day I played with a woman who spent much of her time in working in a local day-care center for children whose mothers had to work. She was looking for volunteer help and I was overjoyed at the thought of repeating my Junior Village experience with small children who needed love and care.

Days when Leland played golf I had freedom and time for myself. Friends, and I was finding among a large acquaintance those I particularly liked, might drop in for tea in the afternoon. There were various responsibilities in shopping or tasks around the home I preferred doing by myself. Again, having time apart made it much easier for us to be together later.

Living so close to the country, I gradually discovered new experiences to replace the different ones I had in the city—beautiful open scenery, blue skies, clean air, trees and many, many birds. A few of the women I knew were dedicated bird-watchers and there were times when I went on walks with them to see if we could locate other birds. I learned a great deal in an area in which previously I had had little concern. In Georgetown our backyard was tiny, like most Georgetown houses, and I had enjoyed taking care of the plantings the limited space would permit. In our new home there was much more space and I became deeply involved in developing a beautiful flower garden and later a small vegetable garden.

There were always so many evening parties that we had all the so-cialization we needed. So I found that my days were full and involv-ing. The greater leisure Leland and I had to talk added to my fulfill-ment. While there was much that I still missed from the past, and while this transition to a new phase in life looked like it would con-tinue, I found that by coming to know myself more fully and honest-ly, by seeking to develop my internal strength and resources and by actively seeking friends rather than sitting back waiting for others to come to me, I was gradually creating a rich period in life for myself.

To go back to my talks with other wives, I found that my openness in discussing my problems in retirement often unleashed other wom-en to talk about theirs. While I found many women who had made successful adjustments to retirement, there were others who were hiding behind pleasant smiles, unhappy feelings and difficulties in relating to their husbands in the closer living together than they had before in the marriage. I heard an amazing number of stories.

Coming through many of the stories were the separate worlds and different expectations for men and women, particularly for my gen-eration. Women were supposed to be more submissive, less in-formed except about home and family, while men were supposed to be stronger, the deciders and protectors. After all, the wife bore his name and took part of her identity from his position in life. These stereotypes, all too frequently incorrect, created a separateness that served as a block to full communication between husband and wife.

In almost all of the stories inadequate communication in the pres-ent resulted from a pattern throughout a long married life and was at the heart of the problem. One woman told me she and her husband had come to North Carolina because her husband was an excellent golfer. She played, but not very well. He was aware that it was his de-sire, more than hers, that brought them here when he retired. He felt it only right that he show his appreciation by playing with her every Sunday. It was a day of torture for her. After every shot she made he offered a critical comment in an effort to improve her game. "Haven't I told you to hold your hands differently?" "You're just swinging your arms instead of pivoting."

After each correction she tensed up and consequently played more poorly, bringing further caustic comments to increase her ten-sion. Sometimes she would flair up in frustration, but she could never talk over with him her full feelings. She told me she was aware that he was trying to be good to her and she didn't have the heart to tell him she hated the Sunday golf outing. So she continued to endure the torture.

One story haunted me for some time because it was such a vivid picture of a misspent life and a spoiled marriage that made retirement unhappy for both wife and husband. I didn't get the story in one piece. Bits were revealed in different talks. The revelations started, after we had become quite friendly, by my describing how lost I had felt when David first entered school and how I had to make myself find other activities to replace the loss I felt. She then told me that before she was married she was well trained technically and would not have had much difficulty in working as much as she wished. When her youngest child went to school, she desperately wanted to return to her vocation for a few hours a day. But her husband was adamant in refusing to allow her to do it. He felt he was on the way to the top of his company and he was afraid that if word leaked out that his wife was working it would look as if he couldn't manage his income and this would hurt his future chances for advancement. She told me she argued with him at the time but he refused to consider her desires. So she gave up all thought of using her training and frittered away her empty hours. She admitted she felt quite hostile about the way his ambition to get to the top disregarded her need to feel useful and to be stimulated.

Later she told me more about her life. Her husband had succeeded in gaining more responsibility and prominence, and in the process had continued to grow as a person. She, on the other hand, had done very little with her life—bridge, luncheons, caring for the home. She finally, hesitatingly, told me that she and her husband had little to say to each other now that they were retired. She knew he was bored with her after the stimulating people he had known. Now they were just living out their lives with little relationship between them. She bitterly blamed herself for giving in to her husband long ago when she had wanted to return to her career.

Not all the stories were like these. I heard of many situations in which wives had developed careers or found worthwhile rewarding activities to keep themselves growing and to replace the lessening demands of children. But most common in all the conversations I held, and the one I most desperately feared before we retired, were stories of difficulties in relationships in the marriage, or of poor communications, resulting from closer living.

Hence, I encountered more problems in retirement than I expected. Working through them with Leland both aided me and immeasurably strengthened our relationship.

But I would be giving the wrong impression if I have implied that we solved all our problems once and for all, and that our relationship from then on remained smooth, harmonious and in a permanent state of bliss.

Just recently we experienced an episode that took weeks to solve. It concerned our returning to Maine to spend the summer away from the heat of North Carolina. During the previous summer in Maine, Leland had been irritable, uncooperative and unfriendly to others. He had sworn never to go back to Maine and I had said I never again wanted him to, but would go by myself.

But in late June of the next summer we talked about our going up to Maine together. I had already made tentative plans with a friend to accompany me to Maine and now I cancelled them. Friends in North Carolina had been under the impression that Leland would stay there and that I would go to Maine. June came and went and still I remained in North Carolina. Our answers to questions of our friends about our plans were vague. Finally we said we both would go.

Then, one morning at breakfast, Leland asked, out of the blue, "Are you really leveling with me about your willingness to have me go with you to Maine? Remember the difficult time I made for you last summer?"

I heard him saying he didn't want to go, after I had changed my plans. I became extremely angry and said, "You stay here all summer and don't bring the subject up again."

We were both too angry at this point to do any "talking through." I called my friend and remade our plans. We told friends in North Carolina that Leland would stay and I would go sometime in late July.

An extreme heat wave struck North Carolina and stayed and stayed. We would play golf very early in the morning and still come home exhausted by the heat. One early morning, after only nine holes of golf, we were drenched in perspiration. Leland looked at me. He must have read something in my face because he said, "This is crazy. Let's go to Maine."

I agreed. We cancelled golf dates, packed, closed the house and left in three days.

We talked through our poor communication and our anger as we drove north. We hope this problem won't occur again but it may. Certainly there will be others, but we learn from each experience and strengthen our relationship each time.

Chapter 3

Marriage in Retirement

One person said to us, "No one knows the bruising many husbands and wives give each other when they retire."

Another told us, "We are like strangers in our marriage going through a ritual without meaning."

We didn't find our marriage to be like the ones cited above, although we certainly discovered how many areas of our relationship could be benefited by review and renewal. We found them difficult to work on. Over the long years of our marriage there had been other times when we had felt the need for readjustments and, as a result, to undergo a process of renewal. *When we retired and found ourselves living more hours a day together than before, our need for renewal became particularly important.*

We had learned earlier the continuing delicate balance of interaction upon which the endurance of a healthy marriage depended. We had long realized that the words, "'til death do us part" held an extremely static connotation, whereas marriage is perhaps the most dynamic process of living in all life. It is only when marriage is viewed as unchanging that partners live like strangers to each other.

That is why we were particularly pleased with the wedding of a daughter of old friends. The minister, before beginning the traditional service, had these words to say to the expectant couple as they stood before him in the company of relatives and friends seated on the large and lovely lawn. He said, in essence, "You, Barbara, and you, Peter, have jointly decided to become one in another. Yet you

have said that at the heart of your contract, each will remain a separate person respecting the other's differences as equal to your own
and that you have pledged yourselves to help each other grow as
unique, fulfilled and worthwhile individuals. So, side by side, freely
sharing your feelings and experiences with each other, you will
endeavor to become equally competent persons, capable of supporting the other, as you are yet joining together as one."

The minister continued, "You, Barbara and you, Peter, have said
that neither wishes to dominate the other but to form a union of
equal persons so that each may reach toward his potentiality and
increase in self-respect. You plan to use the binding force of love,
caring, free communication and sharing of feelings. You plan to
confront your problems together, both openly and realistically, without recriminations, so you may both grow through their solutions.
You have pledged to each other that you will review and renew your
marriage from time to time and as circumstances dictate so that your
marriage remains open and healthy."

How wonderful, we thought, that Barbara and Peter at their young
age should recognize how fluid and changing a marriage is. It had
taken us, in our generation, some time to understand how the winds
of external forces could alter the relationships in marriage. We had
to learn how difficult it was not to form stereotypic pictures and
habitual responses to the other. For many it must take the suddenness of spending time together to become aware of characteristics of
the other unnoticed before.

It is only when marriages have become so static and habitual that
previously unsolved problems, submerged resentments, and punishing and controlling patterns of interaction create at retirement bruising behavior, like the situation of strangers carrying out the formal
rituals of a marriage.

When we retired we slowly discovered, sometimes painfully and
certainly with difficulties, that we needed to renew and rebuild our
marriage and our relationship with each other on a very different
basis than was present before.

We found we needed to subordinate our previous complementary
roles—one as provider and the other as keeper of the home—to a
mutual pattern of caring, understanding, effective communication
and companionship. This was easier said than done because socially-

sanctioned sex and work roles carry a tremendous emotional loading and have much to do with how one sees his or her identity. If the husband should feel his male identity is demeaned by doing household chores, he may lose self-esteem. If the wife feels her workload unnecessarily increased, her hours confined or her house responsibilities criticized, resentment will follow.

We realized that maintaining rigidly separate roles, different status, and superior-subordinate relations would only bring us trouble.

We recognized that Leland's career was essentially halted and that Martha's load of managing the home needed some alleviation so that she, also, could enjoy more leisure. With more time together and fewer work interruptions, we could spend more time in talking together. The immediate problem was what to talk about during the hours at our disposal. Our communications had usually been easy and open, but previously each of us was sufficiently busy that the time for long talks was limited. Now we were supposed to talk at length. But about what? Made conversation? Superficial communication? Gossip about others?

Leland was reminded of a man in a training group. After a number of days he announced to the group that he now knew the difference between conversation and communication.

We needed to communicate, not merely converse. Over leisurely breakfasts we began to share many thoughts that there hadn't been time to share before. Like ice slowly melting, each time we were together there seemed more to share and conversation turned gradually into communication. Each spoke of serious innermost thoughts and each *listened* carefully.

There were other adjustments to talk through so neither felt put-upon or made to sacrifice unwillingly. These adjustments came slowly to ensure our relations would not be damaged. We needed to develop and agree upon a process so we could make changes in our adjustments when new conditions arose.

We talked about the important ingredients of this process. One day, after plenty of discussion, we wrote them down on a sheet of paper. These ingredients were not to be considered as rigid rules to follow but rather to make certain we were in full agreement and to serve as reminders. (Neither of us likes written rules. We are aware

how confining and guilt producing they can be. We merely wished
for some fluid guideposts.) Our list was small but we thought the
content crucial:

1. That when either felt a plan constricting, feelings could be discussed without defensiveness by the other.
2. That each could feel free to bring new situations out in the open to
   be discussed calmly and with no concern that hurt, anger or quarrels would result.
3. That we could talk about how well our plans to provide equal satisfaction and freedom to each were working. Any changes or modifi-
   cations required could be developed on the basis of openly shared
   feelings.
4. That thoughts and feelings of one mate should be shared with the
   awareness that the other partner was interested. Bottled-up feelings,
   we knew, led only to increased hostility.

We realized we should talk out, as the previous chapters indicated,
what part each should take in caring for the house. It was important
to share the unhappy feelings each of us was having for different reasons and receive sympathetic and empathic understanding and help.
Because we were together more, we knew we should discuss the need
each had for privacy and alone-time, and the necessity to be sensitive
to these desires so we didn't intrude on the other at the wrong time.
We recognized we should seek new areas of activities and enjoyment
we could experience together. Taking pleasure in hearing about the
other's activities was a supportive form of sharing. We should know
those activities the other wished to do alone or with others without
feeling rejected. Slowly, gradually and continuously, because we
knew relationships are never static, we discussed many aspects of our
new relations in retirement.

This renewal of our marriage turned out to be more important
than any other renewal process we had experienced before, both for
our marriage and for the well-being of each of us. Most of the conditions of our life in the past remained the same—we retained many individual role tasks. This renewal opened up a wide variety of new
areas to be faced to set a new direction for our relationship. With
many of the purposes of work, of raising a family and of securing
some financial security finished, the major purpose of our marriage
was to be most caring, helpful and compatible with each other.
While these purposes had been present before, now they were su-

preme. To make certain they were present, our long discussions enabling us to recognize these new marital goals and to discover ways of maintaining them were crucial. Otherwise we could have become strangers making the socially appropriate moves.

During our talks we were able to identify clearly those behaviors, important for all human relationships, but particularly important for our own relations now that we were retired.

1. Attentive listening, not easy to accomplish, and empathic understanding requiring the ability to feel as the other feels.
2. Sensitivity to the feelings, moods, desires, needs, wants of the other.
3. Communication of true feelings uninhibited by fear of rejection, defensiveness or conflict.
4. Caring concern for the problems faced by the other and efforts to prevent one's own behavior from adding to these problems.
5. Responsive, stimulative and authentic sharing of individual feelings.
6. Emotional support and help to enable the other to handle problems and adjust to change.
7. Resolving past conflicts so that present problems can be met.

Undoubtedly other guides could be added, but for us the adherence of these would help us revitalize and renew our marriage for our new life in retirement.

Observing Other Couples

During and after our own long renewal discussions, we observed other retired couples as well as we could, noting behaviors toward each partner and occasionally listening to stories wives told Martha.

Many couples seemed to have made excellent transitions to their retirement. We saw evidence of the care, sensitivity, lack of subtle punishing remarks, and companionship that should now be the prime target for the marriage. Before couples had built together for the future of others in the family. Now it should be for themselves.

These couples, as far as we could judge, seemed to be doing well and we could only speculate as to what went on when no one else was present. But there were many other couples who exhibited in various behaviors that they had made no effective transition in their marriage and certainly no thoughtful and planned renewal.

Perhaps one of the saddest pictures of the death of communication between married partners and the emptiness of two lives at re-

They use, throughout, illustrations from observing friends.

tirement was shown to us recently. The two persons in question were old friends. While we had lived in different cities, we saw them sufficiently often so that we could sense a slow deterioration in their lives.

Not long ago they unexpectedly visited us. Unfortunately, during the first day of their visit we were unavoidably busy—one had an engagement that couldn't be broken without upsetting a number of people and the other had office work that had to be completed that day. Our friends, to our regret, had to be on their own for the day.

Our place in North Carolina offers an opportunity for pleasant walks through shaded woods. Our friends knew other couples in our small village they could call upon. We felt we were not totally deserting them.

In our living room are two large overstuffed chairs separated by a small table and lamp. Reading material lies on the table. The chairs, nearly side by side, face in the same general direction. Before we busied ourselves, our two visitors were seated in the two comfortable chairs.

Leland, while working in his study, became acutely aware of prolonged silence. He assumed that the visitors were reading some of the magazines available on the small table separating them. Periodically he entered the living room for a brief comment. Each time he found them sitting silently, not reading, each staring ahead. To his suggestions of a walk or visit to nearby friends, only noncommittal responses occurred.

The sadness of two persons, long married, sitting silently and making no effort to do anything for themselves, was heartbreaking. It was a picture of two persons reaching an end, with empty lives and an unsharing, uncommunicative marriage.

The Maintenance of Rigid Sex Roles: His and Hers

We discovered a number of couples in which the rigid sex roles and divisions of responsibility were tenaciously held to, even though their need had long since passed. The interior of the house was the wife's domain and the decisions all hers. Things outside the house— the car, tools, plants, lawn—fell under the husband's jurisdiction which the wife was not to question. If a new automobile, in his judgment, was needed, he made the decision.

In one incident we knew about the wife had the davenport re-

covered in a pattern that suited her. It never occurred to her to involve him or share her decision to re-cover the furniture with him.
He hated the pattern she chose but said nothing because the decisions about the house were obviously hers and did not concern him.
It was only to friends that he mentioned his dislike of the new
pattern.

While one purpose in continuing definitive sex boundaries, functional perhaps when each had different task responsibilities, was to
maintain and bolster identity and self-esteem, in essence it prolonged the two-world differences perceived so commonly to exist between the sexes. Men are supposed to be, and have pressures to so
perceive themselves, as decisive, masterful, strong, smart, fearless
and protectors. Women are expected to be soft, attractive, dependent, more emotional, less competent, and content with the
menial tasks of housekeeping.

This continuation of sex-role differences to the degree of absurdity
prevents the couple from contemplating any review or renewal of
their marriage, limits the areas of communication, decreases understanding, and reinforces stereotypes. It buries hurts and causes hostilities to remain buried.

We recall one story that beautifully illustrated the miscommunication resulting from long-held, deep-rooted beliefs in sex differences
and the threats ensuing when the differences were even subtly attacked. A woman with a new car asked a man, a stranger, "Is this a
six or an eight cylinder car?" He replied, "I don't know anything
more than women do about cars."

They were not aware that they were reacting to stereotypes about
the sexes; each felt resentment toward the other's response. Translated, the messages sent and received were as follows: The woman
was saying, "I, a woman, am not expected to know as much about en-
gines as a man. You, a man, should be able to answer my question."
The man, hearing this message and feeling attacked and deflated because he was unable to fill the supposed masculine image, responded
by using his sterotype of women to punish her for putting him on the
spot.

The two worlds of men and women are kept apart by the rigidly
separate characteristics, abilities and roles supposedly attached to
each sex. The greater the distance between the worlds, the more

stereotypes operate and the less understanding of the individual worlds exists.

We observed put-downs between husband and wife among couples we knew, husbands who felt it undignified for them to do "women's work," who congregated at the club each morning to spend the day with male companionship. On the other hand, we also saw couples who took pleasure in each other's company and who enjoyed long trips together. They appeared to have found companionship and compatibility as a new value in their marriage and thus more satisfaction in their relations.

Learning about Each Other

The many increasing habits that grow with marriage tend to inhibit the knowledge and awareness each partner has of the other. Unless some dramatic change in behavior occurs, each assumes the other is unchanged. Habitual, and thus superficial, perception of the other rejects the possibility of change. In so many marriages there lies buried in each partner a part of a person unknown to the other.

Two simple anecdotes illustrate the lack of knowledge marital partners have of each other. A recent television advertisement has the salesman in a supermarket turn to the wife with her husband standing by. "Madam," says the salesman who is advertising stuffing, "does your husband prefer potatoes or stuffing with his meal?" "Potatoes," the wife responds. The salesman turns to the husband and asks him which he would prefer. The husband responds by indicating stuffing. The wife, in surprise, turns to her husband and says, "I didn't know. Why didn't you tell me?" "You never asked me," the husband responds.

A couple who were close friends of ours were about to build a new house. The architect talked to them about the general plans they had and then asked if each, alone, would list the things wanted in the house and how each wanted it laid out.

They were surprised. They said they knew they were in agreement. The architect persisted, saying he didn't want either to consult the other in the list each made. They finally agreed. To their great surprise, and subsequent learning, they found on comparing their lists that there was only the vaguest similarity between their lists.

Retirement provides time, as we realized, to learn more about each other—previously undiscovered thoughts, feelings, ideas with-held because they were considered unwanted. Such knowledge of each other, as we experienced it, does not come easily or readily, else it would have been known before. The hidden thoughts and feelings are not necessarily hidden because they are shameful or destructive to the ego, but because they are thought to be insignificant or un-interesting to the other.

So a climate of caring, attentive listening and trust needs to be built to enable each partner in the marriage to allow more of himself to be known to the other. The other, in turn, needs to give clear be-havioral evidence in a caring, but not sugary, response that further understanding is not only desirable but wanted. In this way stereo-types about each mate are demolished.

At times habits or behavioral patterns developed from different conditions when each was away from the other during the day, and so unknown to the other, come to light when the husband retires and the two partners see each other in new ways. Sometimes the shock of the fresh knowledge produces righteous indignation and ultimate quarrels.

We knew such a couple. Unfortunately criticism was not intended but was taken, resulting in unsatisfactory explanations, hurt and ulti-mate hostility and a break in communication. The husband, during his long years of work as an executive—work and an office organiza-tion generally unfamiliar to his wife—with the assistance of compe-tent secretaries under his command, was accustomed to having every paper in its proper place, his desk bare at the end of the day, with new messages, mail and appointment lists laid out for him in the morning. When he needed to refer to a past letter it was produced immediately. His type of work and the limited time available made such organization necessary.

At home, while his wife was neat and clean, the presence of chil-dren and the customary clutter of living made such rigid organiza-tion impossible. This was agreeable to him. He didn't expect the home and office to be the same.

Then he retired. He found it difficult. He couldn't always remem-ber where he had placed his now sparser correspondence or whether he had already answered it. He missed the finely-tuned organization he had known and the secretaries who did so much. With no intention to be critical of the way the home was kept, he did repeat to his wife fairly often how much he missed the perfect order of his office. She, who had always felt that she had done a more than competent job in keeping the home neat, perceived his remarks as critical and took affront. She felt she saw a new side of his personality she had not observed before—obsessive neatness. She failed to realize that having become accustomed to all the careful organization in his work, he was almost unconsciously following her around and closing doors and picking up papers. She had intended to do the picking up and had always done so on her own schedule. She felt deflated, irritated, hostile and then openly angry. She didn't like what her new view of this side of her husband was doing to her.

Her anger produced bewilderment in him, then excuses and finally anger in response. Rather than talking about the situation calmly, trying to understand the other's motives and feelings, there was only attack and counterattack, hurt and misunderstandings. Neither listened to nor understood the other. Each felt put-upon.

Marital partners are often blinded to aspects of the other. When circumstances, such as retirement, reveal previously unrecognized behavioral or personality traits of the other, shock, anger and even rejection occur. External circumstances measurably affect the behavior of the individual. A person, unhappy in a job, can show this by demeanor, posture, behavior and even psychosomatic illnesses. When job conditions become happier, changes occur in the individual. Equally, when an individual is involved and busy, awareness of a marital partner may be reduced and blindness to characteristics result.

From what the husband told us, his working career had been vibrant, filled with exciting persons from whom he learned much and was greatly stimulated. His wife had lived a more sedate and contained life. With a small circle of friends who talked mostly about their husbands and women friends, and with daily television programs, her life seemed full. Returning home at night, often exhausted, there was a minimum of conversation between them. Their interests had gone in different directions. If the husband thought about it at all he was glad that his wife seemed contented. He looked for, and saw, no change in her.

Then he retired. Contact with a variety of stimulating persons met through work was ended. He turned now to his wife. He was now astonished to find her interests narrow, her thoughts dull, her conversation unexciting. He was shocked at the change he saw in her. He failed to realize that over the years he had done little to stimulate her, intellectually, nor to test how interesting she could be. After the shock of his disappointment, he sought companionship from men he met.

Communication, Coping with Conflict and Support

Communication—receiving the feeling and meaning of another without distortion—as our observation of others as well as our own experience confirmed, has two values upon which it depends for its effectiveness. Full, open and receptive communication, on the one hand, creates warmth and greater sharing of feelings, ideas and experiences. It is fundamental to the growth and maintenance of marital relations. On the other hand, communications determine the methods by which differences, disagreements and conflicts between partners are handled. These methods quickly become set into patterns which are fixed during marriage unless deliberate periodic reviews, renewals and changes are made. Unless occasionally modified, these patterns become a major block to a happy and satisfying retirement.

Ineffective or almost nonexistent communication (common among many retired couples) leads to each hiding feelings which, if expressed and properly heard, could bring greater understanding of each other. Otherwise emotional isolation exists for both.

Ineffective communications result in unresolved conflicts in which emotions run high and punishment or demeaning of the other becomes the pattern of the day. Such patterns of coping with conflict and expressing emotion are regressive—more adolescent than adult. Being emotionally adult does not mean that feelings are choked back or denied. It does mean that emotions lie within and belong to the individual. If expressed, and that is usually most healthy, it should be as a fact about oneself and not as punishment of the other. "I am feeling angry," rather than, "You are a ———." Bursts of rage, tantrums, and anger at minor events close off effective communications.

In retirement either or both partners may need understanding and support as they struggle with adjustments. When indifference or re-criminations occur instead of support, the gulf widens between the partners.

In our village everyone goes to the post office each day to pick up the mail. It's a wonderful arrangement because friends are met, dates made, news of the day circulated and sometimes serious conversations are held. We encountered a friend who had recently, and unexpectedly, lost a prestigious and well-paying position. Now he was without work. He wanted to talk. It was about his wife and himself. If ever in his life he needed her support, it was now. He had been terribly hurt by the sudden firing and embarrassed when he met others. He expected sympathy and support from his wife, because new positions would not be easy to find at his age in the late fifties. Instead of support, all he received was blame. It was his fault, she had said, that he had lost his position. There was no one else to blame. He had better get another job quickly because she didn't want him around the house.

Her behavior hurt more than losing the position, he told us. He admitted that he and his wife had always had troubles. Arguments and fights were not uncommon, but they had usually patched them up. Now, he felt, there was no way of communicating with her. When he tried to explain to her the intrigues and maneuvers in his organization that had led to his ousting, she made no attempt to listen or understand. She showed no sympathy for his anxiety about the future.

There was little we could say except to express our regret, but what came through to us was the result of a long period of poor communications in the family, leading now to her punishing him for assumed hurts she had experienced before.

As one or both partners in a marriage are unable or unwilling to talk through a conflict, an emotional blow-up exists and continues, hostility increases for both and the area of conflict is either dealt with by petty remarks or careful avoidance of the area. The result is two-fold. An entire area becomes too painful to touch or is only productive of further conflict. Further, this emotional region is walled off, and the possibility of solving the existing problem is lost and the ability to solve future problems is diminished. When retirement arrives, only the simplest of problems, carrying no adverse emotional reactions, are possible of being resolved.

Two simple stories illustrate different aspects of such noncommunication. A wife told Martha that when a difference arose between her husband and herself and her own anger came to the fore, her husband merely walked out of the room or house, slamming the door, indicating, to her, his disgust at her anger, his inability to handle his own, and giving her no release from her anger by talking through the problem. As a result her anger increased. When he returned, he acted as if the incident had never occurred, leaving the cause unsolved to erupt at another time. If, on his return, she tried again to bring up the problem, endeavoring to explain what his walking away was doing to her, he only repeated his former behavior. No talking-through took place that would have eased the feelings of both.

Another wife told gleefully how she handled her husband when he became angry at something she had done. Rather than acknowledge the error or talk the matter through, she retired to her room, locked the door and refused to talk to him or to prepare any meals until he apologized. She never considered what this was doing to their relationship or his feelings about himself. Forcing him to humble himself couldn't increase his self-respect or his feeling towards her.

These are examples that would bode ill for compatibility and sharing in retirement. They represent some of the behavior patterns causing couples to live out their lives as basically strangers to each other.

On the other hand, if a habit of talking-through problems and emotional tensions is adopted at any time in a marriage, each can help the other through the transition to retirement. But talking-through, we had found, requires that a number of highly important conditions be met. Being human, they are not easy for any of us.

1. Allowing the other to express the feelings bottled up. Give such expression the respect of *listening* without an immediate counter-attack. Otherwise, the feelings, not listened to or rejected, remain to rankle and increase.
2. Recognizing that defensiveness creates reactions of *not* being listened to, with consequent feelings of irritation and futility.
3. Having an opportunity to express one's feelings with the expectation of being listened to, and with as little blame of the other as possible.
4. With feelings released instead of increased, endeavoring together

to seek calmly the causes of the explosion. This requires a joint search instead of an antagonistic argument. Such a joint search adds for each feelings of well-being and fulfillment.

5. Remembering that *it takes two to have a relationship* and that each bears a part of the responsibility for its decline, maintenance or improvement.

6. With causes jointly and calmly sought, plans to prevent the same conflict arising again, a process to handle future conflicts can be developed.

Difficult as these conditions are to meet in the heat of emotion, the alternative presents side-by-side living and minimal sharing and compatibility. Effective talking-through and nondistorted listening eliminates the typical responses of, "You shouldn't feel that way" (when the person does), or, "It doesn't make sense to feel like that" (when feelings, not logic, are the problem) or, "Try forgetting it" (in other words, bury it and don't bother me). Such comments result in experiencing lack of understanding and subsequent buried feelings. Withholding feelings when emphatic understanding is needed brings internal loneliness.

We had to work all this through ourselves to gain a true understanding as part of the review and renewal of our relations. We learned it gradually and with hard and committed effort.

Sensitivity to the Feelings, Needs, Wishes of the Other

We continued to relearn how difficult it was to be truly sensitive to the feelings and desires of the other. Sometimes, in trying to be sensitive we became insensitive. Being oversolicitous of how the other person felt might be irritating to one who merely wished to be alone. Sometimes neither of us did what he wished to do in order to please the other. Such deceptive behavior is often revealed leaving the other partner annoyed. Total sensitivity is seldom accomplished.

Observing other couples we were frequently aware of the degree of insensitivity one mate showed to the other. In some cases one partner, anxious that the other show up well before others, would make corrective remarks in front of a group. Individuals, insensitive to their own motives and behavior, would argue loudly, using "logic" to justify their behavior, to the distress of their mates.

We observed two couples in which the effort to improve the other partner resulted only in unhelpful and insensitive behavior. The wife still smoked, although she would have liked to quit. But her husband reminded her in front of others how bad the habit was and how stubborn she was in maintaining the habit. Her embarrassment was mixed with anger at his insensitivity in making such comments in public. Her only alternative, she felt, was to smoke more.

In another case the situation was reversed. The husband smoked, even after warnings from his doctor. His wife, thinking she was helping, continually reminded him of the doctor's warning. Each time she emptied an ash tray she had a comment to make. Every comment she made added to his difficulty in giving up his habit. These comments increased his hostility toward her. He not only continued to smoke but now deliberately let ashes fall on the rug. The caustic remarks she made as she vacuumed only widened the distance between them. By the time they retired the initial conflict had blossomed into a host of other conflicts. Now, he deliberately did everything she abhorred and urged him not to. She, in turn, increased her punishing comments. She spent as much time away from the house as she could, while he, grateful to be away from her, stayed home more.

A final story, illustrating lack of feeling as well as the gulf between men and women, describes the difficulties—and results—of insensitive remarks or behavior. The husband was a child psychologist, trained not only to understand children's problems but also adults' in relation to children. His wife resented her fourth pregnancy (it was not planned). Her emotional resistance to being pregnant again brought forth feelings against her husband. She complained of the years of confinement still ahead of her. Her husband soothingly said, "Don't feel bad. In another six years, you'll be a free woman." Her anger exploded. She let him know how thoroughly insensitive she thought his remark was. He didn't have to spend six years in raising the child to school age. Fourteen years of steady confinement with one small child after another was no joke. He ought to understand that.

Expectations of What Retirement Will Be Like

Unless couples thoroughly talk through the expectations each has for the retirement period, only trouble is likely to ensue. Such preretirement discussion, and it must be honest and open, needs to include the possibility of change when retirement actually occurs. What before may have seemed desirable, can, in actuality, be less so.

One of our own errors that caused us difficulties later resulted from each of us having different expectations of what retirement would be like. Martha thought it would be an unmitigated disaster. Leland expected it to be a delightful release. Not only did we overly anticipate, but we were far apart in what we expected and wanted.

In talking to other couples we discovered both similar and different reactions. Some, like us, had experienced the husband being certain what he wanted, while his wife really wished for some other retirement plan, but said nothing about her desires. Others, disappointed in what they expected would be an easy transition, blamed the partner for the mistaken expectation. One wife had yearned for years for more of her husband's time. But when they retired she found they had little to share.

We observed three basically different situations among retired couples we knew:

1. Some couples exhibited continued, and increased, sharing of intellectual interests that made their retirement rich in human companionship.
2. Neither partner in other couples continued more than the minimum superficial communication. Neither was interested in any event or conversation that stimulated intellectual growth with the result that their conversation between themselves dealt only with daily mundane activities and local gossip.
3. In the third group of couples, one partner had maintained intellectual curiosity and interest while the other had not. The result was usually minimal communication, withdrawal and subtle demeaning punishments.

When we visited homes we looked to see what books and magazines were about and whether they looked as if they had been read. In homes with reading material we typically encountered couples who welcomed stimulating, wide-ranging conversations. Because each partner added uniquely to the conversation and didn't always agree with the other on each point, we were led to believe that as a couple they stimulated each other with differing but helpful reactions that were not "put-downs." We felt that a deeply interactive, mutually stimulative, and happy marriage in retirement had been reached. Here was caring understanding of each mate. With these couples, we felt, help to each partner could be given and received without hostility, and each partner had found a degree of tranquility.

Recently we received a wonderful letter from an old friend who had known his share of internal struggle with self-image. Among his beautiful lines are the following: "I am in touch with new powers and new rhythms in me. My health has never been better—my blood pressure is back to normal—I am at peace with what I see and now have no need to change me or be what I am not—my being is more tranquil—and I am now—for me—in beautiful uncharted waters."

Whether or not the marriage partners we found who were mutually stimulative had always been so, it was clear to us that these couples were making the retirement period in their lives productive and rewarding to themselves and a time for new growth.

We noticed, in those couples whose reading was obviously minimal and intellectual curiosity almost nonexistent, a restlessness and discontent. Playing games—golf, tennis, cards—and social occasions filled part of their time. But during the many other hours their restlessness was obvious. They needed always to be physically moving. What discontent, self-dislike and unhappiness lay inside each person we could only guess about.

Saddest of all, we thought, was the situation in which one partner had remained intellectually alert and interested. The partner whose intellectual growth had stagnated found little to talk about except gossip about neighbors, and harbored prejudices, unshakable mistaken beliefs and rigid stereotypes about others. The other partner often showed distaste of the mate, made punishing statements, often before others, such as, "You wouldn't understand" or, "That's a silly statement." Hurt, hostility, anger or quarrels seem common in such situations.

One husband whose wife's major interest was soap operas and who showed little interest in anything else, said, "I never thought my life and marriage would end like this."

The three categories of retired couples told us again how important renewal in marriage was if the retirement phase of life was to be active and increasingly companionable for us as a couple.

Bitterness in Retirement

We met individuals who felt bitter at retirement for a variety of reasons. Their bitterness frequently led to blame, punishment and controlling behavior toward their spouses. This was their way of hitting out because of the hurt inside them, and marital happiness and compatibility was impossible.

Bitterness can result from many causes. Dreams of achievement remaining unfulfilled at retirement can lead to blaming circumstances, blaming others, even a partner who is viewed as somehow having blocked the consummation of the dream. Anger that life seems short and aging quick to appear helps to destroy the person. The wife whose girlhood dream of high social standing has not occurred can wonder, often aloud, whether she married the right suitor. She can feel envy of a sister or girl friend whose life has been richer. Bitterness is deeper because blame is difficult to direct toward oneself.

Waning sexual attractiveness and sexual potency may threaten deeply, increasing the fear of old age and death, or lower masculine or feminine self-esteem. Women who feel that diminishing physical beauty makes them less attractive to men may worry that their husbands will be attracted to younger women.

When husband and wife have played the game of seeking upward mobility in social standing, and who continue to use the same status coin without success, bewilderment and bitterness may follow their gradual rejection.

So we discovered restlessness, boredom, loneliness, bitterness and either unwillingness or incapability upon the part of some couples to deal with their transition to a retired state. But we also found those who had achieved sharing, compatibility and tranquility within themselves.

Carry-overs from Preretirement Marriage

When no review or renewal of a marriage takes place just before or during retirement, habitual patterns of interaction between partners, built up over the years, create greater difficulties, because neither one is away from the other for as much time as before. Attention is not distracted by as many outside demands as previously.

We saw many of these patterns in operation among those we knew.

It seems natural and very human to wish to improve, correct and even make over one's marital partner. Perhaps more than is realized, "what others will think" exerts a force. Small corrections, ignored or resisted, bring stronger corrections. Consequently, a pattern of attempt and resistance is created and anger and hostility develop.

It becomes public. "I've told you not to do that." Punishment and counter-punishment results. Defensiveness, rationalization and hostility bury relationships, and communication and sharing diminish.

We viewed so often the extent to which the behavior of each partner impacted upon the other—sometimes helpfully but often in ways producing guilt in the other. And with guilt, as we well knew, comes some reduction in self-esteem and consequent hostility and unhappiness.

From our own long exploration into our transitional problems in retirement, from letters and occasional visits from old friends, and from observations and discussions with those we saw frequently, we became much clearer about three major points:

1. For a serene, self-rewarding and productive retirement, our purpose in marriage needed to shift from our previous role responsibilities to an emphasis upon sharing, communication and companionship.
2. Review and renewal of our marriage, and we've become to believe of many others, is extremely important in the transition to retirement.
3. After all our long hours of sharing and exploration, we listed for ourselves what appeared to be necessary ingredients of a marriage in retirement. They are:
   a. Openness of communication and sharing of feelings.
   b. Trust in the honesty in which each views himself.
   c. Respect for the uniqueness, individuality and identity of the other.
   d. Autonomy and privacy to enlarge personal freedom and growth.
   e. Caring and love. Caring is defined as non-possessive.
   f. Empathy and understanding.
   g. Support for expansion and growth.
   h. Utilization of conflict for improved relations.

A Hypothetical Case Study of Marital Review

The wife had thought for some time about how she could open up a series of discussions with her husband about their imminent retirement. She dreaded making the effort because they had not talked about such problems before, but the alternative of doing nothing was too awful to contemplate. She suspected he was more concerned about his retirement than he told her. He would mention casually the story of some "sad sack" who continued to come to the office seeking companionship after he had retired. Other stories told her retirement was on his mind.

She waited for a propitious time—an evening when they had no obligations and she could leisurely approach the subject. She said, "When you retire things are going to be very different for us. You will be home more than you have been. How will you feel? Wouldn't it be good to talk about what these changes will mean for both of us?"

He replied, "What are you talking about? We'll get along as we always have. What are you discontented about now?"

"I'm not discontented," she said. "I just know life will be different for both of us then, and I think we ought to talk about it and make some plans. You remember the Smiths. They had a very bad time together after he retired. Also, remember our parents. They weren't happy."

"Nonsense," he said abruptly. "I've always taken care of you, haven't I? What are you moaning about?"

She was discouraged by his unwillingness to discuss mutual problems with her, and she felt like giving up. But she became more determined to push ahead with the issue.

"Maybe you don't have any concerns, but I do. Why won't you listen to my feelings just once? I'm the one who will have you underfoot all day messing up my life. It can be fun sharing more time together or it can be sheer misery, and I want to talk about it." She was shocked at her outburst, but she felt she had to get through to him.

He didn't reply right away but looked at her seriously. Then, "I guess you are right" he said slowly. "Perhaps retirement is going to make things quite different. But what do you want to talk about?"

"Us," she said tersely. "What do you think retirement is going to be like for you? What are you looking forward to and what are you dreading? I confess I have some worries concerning this period in my life. How can we plan our lives together so it will be good?"

They took the first step that night. He spoke of some of the things he wanted to do and admitted, grudgingly, and with evidence of fear, that he worried about how he would feel when he didn't have the office to go to—the title and status to hold onto or the influence to ex-

ert on the company's progress. She gained a new insight into his difficulty in suddenly relinquishing all the power and prestige he now
held. She had never quite realized before, because he had always
been so self-contained, how much his identity and feeling about himself was tied up with his work. She knew he had always worked hard
but she had never realized how hard he had driven to reach his present position. She suddenly realized, also, how much her identity was
tied into his. While she wouldn't feel the loss to the extent he would,
the realization helped her to understand him better.

He told her for the first time about his predecessor who had
seemed lost when he retired and who aged very rapidly. He admitted
this worried him. He wanted to avoid this for himself, but he wasn't
certain just how retirement would affect him. Maybe, he admitted,
he would need her help.

They had already decided on where they would live—a recreational place he had always wanted to go to. She hadn't been as crazy
about the idea as he was, but she wasn't violently opposed and so she
had made no objections, although she had a few qualms. After her
husband had talked about some of his concerns, as well as what he
was looking forward to in recreation and leisure, she spoke of her
worries. Moving, for her, meant leaving a cherished home, sorting
out items, holding many memories she couldn't take to a new and
smaller place, leaving a circle of friends of many years, giving up a
round of social and volunteer activities that had made life meaningful, and facing the necessity of creating a nest, a circle of friends, and
meaningful activities somewhere else. By the time she had listed all
of the disengagements or losses she might suffer, her husband was
astonished and overwhelmed. He had been so busy thinking about
his own potential difficulties he had not considered hers. It was an
eye-opener and he became more conscious of the need for joint
thinking through the problems they might face.

Before they stopped for the evening, she also mentioned some of
her concerns about the future, but suggested they think about them
before any more discussion. She said she was worried about his being around the house all day. Would he allow her the freedom she
had grown accustomed to, or would he demand all of her time?
Would he intrude too much on her role of maintaining the house,
thereby depriving her of purposeful activity? She said some women

had told her of situations where the husband, when he retired, took over the house and treated his wife like a maid. That wasn't for her. At the same time would he be sensitive about not adding to her household duties? Was there a good dividing line they could work out that would enable him to help around the house without intrusion? She worried, also, about him. Would he be restless, bored, aimlessly drifting away his life? The last thing she wanted was a husband hanging over her shoulder. When he protested that he would be occupied with his golf, she wondered whether, at his age, he could play every day. What other activities had he planned for himself? He admitted he hadn't thought too much about that.

She raised the question as to how they could strike a proper balance between doing things together and having time for privacy and separation from each other. If either felt they had to be together most of the time, guilt and hostility might occur. There were times, she said, when it was more relaxing to be with women friends and not have to worry about his presence inhibiting conversation. She imagined he would need an equal amount of male companionship in which she was not involved. One of their problems, she thought, was to work out a relationship in which they could have time together and time apart without either feeling guilty or trying to over-possess the other. These were all questions they could discuss later.

This was enough for the first session. They went to bed soberly, thinking about the evening's talk.

Over a number of talk sessions they discussed much of the following:

1. What were the changes they could foresee now that might create emotional or relational problems when they retired? How sensitive could each be to the problems and needs of the other? How could each one help the other?

2. With more leisure time, could they plan to get better acquainted with each other and to share more with each other? Was a leisurely breakfast the best time for long talks? Or other times?

3. What tasks could each take responsibility for in the home to provide sufficient sharing without taking away long-held roles from the other? If such preplanning were not done, the common comment, "If I didn't do it, it wouldn't be done," would occur.

4. Could each plan sufficient personal activities that one wouldn't become overly dependent upon the other for companionship and things to do?

5. What approaches and methods could they use to resolve problems and disputes better than they had in the past? Needing each other more now, could they learn to communicate more openly and fully?
6. How could they prevent defensiveness or recriminations from sharing feelings with each other? If either felt infringed upon how could this be brought into the open without causing hurt?

This hypothetical couple, starting with initial resistance to discussing potential future problems, overcame it through months of discussion and laid the groundwork for their retirement. The longer they carried on the discussion, the closer they felt toward each other. They found they were sharing feelings far more than they had for years. Both felt satisfaction with themselves and each other, and each gained a sense of self-fulfillment. But this couple had an extremely important ingredient going for them. Each one felt sufficient self-worth and self-esteem that searching questions about their relations could be faced. Each could take information about personal behavior from the other without undue defensiveness. They felt sufficient self-worth that they could tackle problems together. If either had lacked sufficient self-esteem the situation would have been very different. There would have been a refusal to discuss the issue for fear of losing authority or exposing behavior, or there would have been submissiveness and willingness on the part of one to agree to whatever the other decided. Self-esteem upon the part of both partners is necessary if open, honest interaction is to occur.

After retirement, when the experience brings unforeseen and unexpected problems, is an important time for a further review of marital relations. Unanticipated irritants can escalate into major emotional issues. One may feel called to overly sacrifice time and attention. Living in retirement usually is very different than patterns of living experienced before. New and different concerns, societal pressures to feel separated from much of the world, problems of approaching aging, the increasing possibility of the mate dying with unique social and emotional difficulties all speak to the desirability of a marital review and possible readjustment of relationships between partners. Only then will there be the likelihood that the period of being elderly in marriage in retirement can be a happy, contented, self-rewarding phase in the total span of life.

Questions for a Marital Check-Up

1. Have either of us felt there were times recently when we held back our feelings, ideas or desires? What were the situations? Why did we hold back? What were the consequences of not being fully open? What did the other do that helped to create the decision to hold back? Not listen? Appear defensive? Did holding back make it necessary or desirable to hold back again?

2. Were there times when one of us felt the other wasn't really listening? What were the occasions? How did the other show nonlistening? What did the lack of listening do to the relationship? Why wasn't the other listening? How, in the future, can either of us indicate a feeling that the partner isn't listening without causing defensiveness?

3. Were there times recently when either one of us seemed insensitive to the feelings of the other? When did these situations occur? How was the insensitivity shown? What did it do to the other and to further communication?

4. Were there times recently when either of us felt the other was punishing, rejecting or "putting-down"? What actions or behavior left this feeling? What were the circumstances leading up to the behavior? How did the other respond? By hiding hurt feelings? By showing anger? By punishing back? Is there any residual feeling left that should be expressed to clear the air? What can be done in the future if either feels punished or hurt by the other?

5. Were there behaviors of either of us irritating to the other that were not mentioned at the time, or continued though mentioned? What little things are irritating but not to the point of saying anything?

6. Were there times recently when either said yes when no was strongly felt? Why was this so? Fear of conflict? Pressure? What?

7. Were there times when either of us felt misunderstood, but didn't say so? Why not? What blocked response? What can we do in the future if either of us feels misunderstood?

8. When we have differences or conflicts, how do we handle them? By fighting? By one giving in? Do we really listen to the other in a conflict or is each of us too anxious to defend or punish the other? Do we try to understand how the other feels? In the future can we develop a better method of solving differences so both of us feel satisfied?

9. Did either of us overcrowd the other when the other wanted privacy? What were the occasions? How was the problem handled? How could such situations be handled better without causing hurt or feelings of lack of caring or rejection?

10. What are the ways either of us think will help to improve our relationship? What changes or efforts will it take by both of us?

11. Have either of us consciously helped the other to grow and feel more self-fulfilled? What were the occasions? How was encouragement and help given? How conscious has either of us been of the need for the other to feel self-fulfilled? What are the cues that would enable each of us to know when encouragement to extend oneself is needed? How can help be given without pressure, smugness, patronizing or punishing?

Part Two

Coping with the Problems

Introduction

We wrote about our trials and tribulations in being retired in Part 1 of this book because it appeared to be the most realistic and convincing way of illustrating the troubles that could be encountered. We added incidents and examples about others we knew, met, observed, listened to, and heard about to augment our personal experiences. If we, who have professional training and long experience in teaching others about human behavior, still encountered troubles in adjustment, made mistakes, made oversights in preplanning and had struggles in the transition, it's no wonder that so many people without our specialized professional background have such tremendous problems making the passage from active working lives into retirement. All the more reason, then, that many of the increasing number of persons now retiring must become more aware, alert, and prepared to deal with the problems of retirement.

Although we never thought the system we evolved through our odyssey represented the perfect way to meet and solve all retirement problems for everyone, we do hope our discoveries about ourselves, each other, our marriage and better ways of resolving inevitable differences and disagreements could lead others to consider more seriously the emotional and relationship problems inextricably bound up in any transition to retirement.

Our adventures made us clearly aware of three basic requirements to be met so that emotional and relational problems in this phase of life can be worked through to achieve happiness, sharing, compatibility, companionship, continued intellectual growth and individual tranquility. They are:

1. The thorough, open review, renewal, and adaptation of many aspects of the relationship between husband and wife to meet the new situations retirement provides.

2. The achievement by each person of a high degree of self-acceptance and self-liking (as opposed to the amount of self-dislike so many persons hold), self-esteem, self-respect and a sense of self-worthiness. The attainment of as much self-awareness as possible to become "free at last" (to quote Dr. Martin Luther King, Jr.) from the pressure to be something one is not. To come to know oneself without low opinion or dislike of oneself and to have the courage and dignity to be oneself without pretense, guilt or shame. Freedom from self-dislike and ability to discard a mask and be oneself is quickly recognized and appreciated by others.

3. The improvement of the relations and communications between marriage partners to prevent destructive hurt and conflict, to establish empathic understanding, and to aid in the growth of sensitivity and support for the development and strengthening of the other.

Each of these requirements is highly complex and composed of many understandings and skills, is difficult to achieve, and intertwines with the others. No one requirement stands by itself. If, for example, one partner does not feel free to be honest and is repressed by the other, no effective collaborative review and renewal of the marital relationship is likely to occur. A partner feeling insecure and submissive may resist a review lest it open up areas in which one feels inadequate. When both partners possess sufficient self-understanding and internal strength to accept and respect themselves and are free from defensiveness or fear, they can collaborate equally in examining their relationships.

If such a full and honest review and renewal of their marriage, with necessary improvements, is not held, little hope is present for change in habitual, and often insensitively harmful, patterns of relations and communications. Old patterns persist and become more damaging and destructive.

With no improvement in communications or relationships, neither partner is helped to overcome feelings of inadequacy or self-dislike. Such feelings prevent shared thoughts. Even when one partner accepts himself and experiences self-esteem while the other does not, an effective marital review is difficult. When both partners fall short of adequate self-liking and self-respect, such a review, if held, usually becomes a punishing interchange.

Hence a marital review, renewal and necessary adaptations, so tremendously important in retirement, if successful adjustments are to be made, is based upon self-understanding and self-acceptance by

both partners. The review, in addition, can bring greater understanding to each partner. The result can be empathic understanding
and support for each other, rather than the semihostile side-by-side
living common among many couples.

How these interactive requirements can be secured by individuals
and couples becomes the basis of Part 2 of this book. The struggles
we endured and the intensive efforts toward our own growth that we
undertook can be better understood as a result of this section.

Chapter 4

Getting to Know and Accept Yourself

Our little grandchildren were riding in the car with Martha. Jeffrey, who was six, said, "I love you first and me second." But Kendra, at four, wrinkled her brow and said thoughtfully, "I love me first and you second."

Fortunately Jeffrey, as a small child, spoke from a momentary overabundant love for Martha. Otherwise, if that statement represented his usual image of himself, he would have been less emotionally healthy than Kendra. He would already have learned that there were parts of himself he did not like, but could not talk about. He would have wanted to be someone else rather than himself. He would have been demeaning himself, admitting he was not all he thought he should be. He might have been learning to flatter in order to be liked because he wasn't entirely sure he was liked for himself. He might have begun to hide parts of his inner self for fear of disapproval.

Instead of becoming self-determining and endeavoring to reach his potentials, he would have tried to be like others. The continuing dislike of himself could turn to envy and hostility to others. His dislike of himself could increase and cause him to expect failure, and so experience it through much of his life. He would not believe himself to be as capable as he potentially was. Throughout life he would wear a mask portraying what he thought others would approve of rather than being himself. He would often say yes when he meant no and dislike himself for doing so.

Fortunately, over the subsequent years, Jeffrey has shown no evidence of self-dislike. Rather, he shows behavioral proof of self-acceptance and a healthy personality.

The Introduction to Part 2 indicated the importance of a marital review, renewal and necessary adaptations to fit the new conditions of retirement. The Introduction made it clear that for a collaborative review to be effective and helpful, both partners should have sufficient self-liking and self-respect and should accept themselves and each other. Otherwise one or both might be too insecure and lack internal strength great enough to undergo an honest and candid examination of their previous patterns of relationships and of changes in their relationships that retirement might require. Self-awareness, self-respect, self-esteem upon the part of both, in turn, determine how effectively and deeply they communicate, and how sensitively they understand, support and help each other. Hence the major conditions of a marital review—self-liking and self-awareness and effective communication and sensitive support—are interwoven and mutually supportive.

The vital transition period of retirement provides an ideal time when these interweaving factors can be confronted. The sudden changes in work responsibilities for husbands produce leisure time and tremendous personal need to come to terms with oneself; to become aware of motives and emotions, to discover the basic being now stripped of outer symbols, to assess old values and find new ones, to seek different ego-satisfying activities to replace those no longer possible, and to become more open.

Retirement inevitably raises the probability of changes in marital relations. With leisure and face-to-face living and the marriage stripped of outside responsibilities, partners may rediscover each other, find joy in companionship and realize the stimulation for growth each can give the other.

Basic is self-liking (far different from conceit which usually contains some insecurity), self-acceptance and ease with oneself. These are not achieved readily. Many pressures in life produce self-destructive motives and actions, and the immobilization resulting from self-dislike. If retirement can be used to free oneself from self-doubt, motivations leading to self-fulfillment can develop.

Self-Dislike and How It Grows

The seeds of self-dislike are usually planted early in childhood with "don'ts" and "bads" and "oughts" and "shoulds." They are watered by comparisons with siblings or other children. They find fertile climate in mistakes and small failures. In childhood and adolescence, lack of popularity and scarcity of friends, awkwardness and lessened physical attractiveness, obesity or physical infirmities or unsuccessful school efforts increase self-dislike. Marriage to an overbearing spouse or lack of success in work ventures confirms self-doubt and self-dislike. Further failures and put-downs are expected and realized.

So, by the time of retirement, the individual, convinced of inadequacy, does little to change or develop his potentials. Fear of discovery of one's inadequacies is exhausting. The tragedy of self-dislike, or lack of self-respect, lies in the assumption accepted by the individual that to be less than perfect is a personal fault for which one should feel shame. Yet, if all were perfect, all would be alike—stamped from the same mold without uniqueness, individuality or personal identity. What occurs is that those (and they are many) with self-doubt and lack of a sense of worthiness do little or nothing to increase their potentials or build on their unique aspects. Their psychic energies are spent in hiding their seeming inadequacies and their feelings about themselves are unhappy and painful.

Retirement (or the planning for it) can be a period of joylessness, unhappiness and self-recrimination or it can become a phase in life when happiness, productivity, self-fulfilling activity and tranquility are possible. One of the major keys to such a rewarding time is greater self-awareness. It is a time when each individual, freed from many of the constrictions of the early and middle years, can look deeply and honestly at oneself to clear away misconceptions and erroneous doubts about oneself. Self-awareness can lead to self-acceptance and self-respect.

Good mental and emotional health requires self-liking rather than self-disliking, feelings of worthiness rather than unworthiness, self-respect as opposed to self-disrespect, internal security and internal strength rather than insecurity and internal fear. Increased self-knowledge leading to increased self-acceptance brings internal freedom and tranquility.

Self-dislike, on the other hand, serves as a destructive growth in the self leading to fear of oneself, immobilization of behavior, hiding behind a mask, fearing discovery, and rejection of self-awareness.

Self-Dislike: What Sustains It and What It Causes

One of the major sustaining forces of self-dislike results from the misconceptions individuals have learned or have been taught about their emotions. From early childhood, rages and explosions of anger were "no no's" to be punished if continued. Males were taught that expressions of the softer emotions were to be inhibited. As a result, many of the emotional aspects of life present a dark, forbidding area not to be understood but to be endured. Yet emotions provide much of the psychic energy for action as well as much of its joy and exhilaration.

It is difficult for many persons to realize and accept the fact that they own their emotions—that they create and cause them. It is far more customary to say, "You made me angry" than to say, "I have created anger within me and have decided to accuse you of triggering its expression." Or, "I have filled myself with anger which really may be directed toward myself, but this I would find difficult to admit." Or, "Your disagreement threatens my beliefs."

Persons without keen self-awareness would have great difficulty in realizing that they have chosen to be angry or hostile or unhappy rather than being made so by an outside event or person. They would find it hard to understand why they should seek the cause of their decision. Who has not experienced the situation of being deeply upset at an event or a person one day, yet totally without reaction to the same event or person another day. In such cases, was the emotion caused or created by the outside agent or was the decision made to generate the emotion by the person himself?

When the individual says, "You made me angry," he directs blame toward the other and absolves himself. When the individual can say, "I chose to feel angry," the question as to why the choice was made can be raised. Motivation for self-understanding and growth occurs. In the first instance no learning takes place because the individual assumes no personal responsibility for the emotion.

One may be at peace, filled with pleasant feelings. Some event— the action or expression of another person, stubbing a toe, experiencing the breaking of a bag of groceries while carrying it, a flat tire— can cause the pleasant, peaceful feelings to be changed by the person involved to angry, frustrating, hostile feelings. The blame is directed outward—to the other person, to someone leaving an object one trips over, to the manufacturer of grocery bags or the clerk at the store, or to the tire manufacturer.

It is not wrong to create within oneself frustrated, hostile, angry feelings suddenly replacing peaceful and pleasant ones. Everyone does it. What is dreadfully wrong is to deny the creation and owner-ship of these emotions and to blame it on another. It's a case of, "You made me very angry" vs. "I have filled myself full of anger, and it can be helpful to our relations for you to know why I did this to myself."

Some individuals with self-dislike and many insecurities carry a la-tent, smoldering emotion within themselves without always being aware they are doing so. They are often known as "angry persons." Their self-hate and self-anger look for targets to pour forth the hate and anger that they cannot accept for themselves.

One man who fancied himself an excellent tennis player and who usually played an acceptable game lost an important match he could have won easily. Later he told all and sundry that the loss was caused by a single remark someone in the audience had made to him just before the game. The remark made him so angry, he said, that he couldn't control himself during the match. He would have totally re-jected the thought that he was an angry man, or that he merely used the excuse of the innocuous statement to release the anger within him which destroyed his game.

Lack of understanding and awareness of one's motives result in failure to seek knowledge about oneself. Adoptions of rationalized reasons rewarding the self provide yet another sustaining force pre-venting self-awareness and increasing self-doubt.

The parent punishing the child, may say (and believe), "This hurts me, but I must teach you to behave." Another motive may be a threat to the authority of the parent, a challenge to the right to con-trol, or fear of social censure.

The continued use of secondary motives may lead others to have less trust in the person and so withhold complete acceptance. This lack of trust communicates to the individual and serves to sustain self-dislike, further covered up by more expressions of self-reward-ing motives.

One of the more difficult problems people face is to separate their behavior from their real selves. Failing to understand that various motives affect any specific act or expression and that self-created emotions intrude on behavior, individuals disliking some of their behavior, and sensing disapproval from others, learn to dislike themselves. It is an easy step to dislike another if the behavior or even thoughts of the other are disliked. If behavior can be viewed as a single aspect of the total self, subject to modification or change, then self-acceptance of one's uniqueness is possible because of the realization that all exist within a common human circumstance, and need to improve.

When behavior is equated with self, tremendous pressures are felt to behave, believe and be what others approve, all at the denial of self. Endeavoring to be what others desire creates internal tension, inhibits internal freedom, prevents internal tranquility and atrophies creativity. Equating behavior with self produces self-blame, self-disparagement and possible self-dislike. Self-dislike, in turn, makes honest, effective, collaborative relations with others difficult to maintain.

Self-dislike reduces the individual. Feelings of confidence and competency are diminished. Such feelings as, "I can't do that," "Why try?" and "Others are better" are inhibiting forces to action and growth. As one feels lowered in self-worthiness, envy of others may occur. Factors one dislikes in himself are disliked in others. Reduction in self-esteem can create anger directed at oneself and toward others.

Self-dislike walls off self-examination and prevents self-understanding. What is disliked in yourself is typically feared to be only the "tip of the iceberg." So much more that is "bad" could be discovered if one looked, that the tendency is to hide as much of the tip as possible and make little effort to improve or change.

Disliking yourself is painful. Feeling the pain of self-dislike makes it easier to punish others for one's own disliked parts. Feeling the tension of self-dislike makes it difficult to understand the feelings of others. Self-dislike contributes to insensitivity. Feeling unworthy causes one to be other than oneself.

Self-dislike prevents or distorts the equality of contributions necessary for an effective marital review. The partner with a sense of low self-worth may submissively follow the ideas of the other partner because his own contributions would be viewed as valueless. As an opposite reaction, fearing that such an examination might merely uncover more faults, the self-doubting partner might refuse to engage in a review of relations. A third reaction is possible. The spouse undergoing the pain of what he feels is his inadequacy might use the review to reduce the perceived superiority of the other through punishing comments.

Individuals experiencing extreme self-doubt, lack of self-esteem, lack of self-respect and feelings of unworthiness seek evidence to maintain these feelings, resist efforts toward understanding the complexities of their being and suffer the anguish of insecurity and anxiety. They are neither free to be themselves and open with others, nor do they experience a sense of well-being and spontaneity. Fearful of revealment, their relations with others tend to be formal, distant, dependent or punitive. Full companionship is limited. Lacking respect for themselves, they find difficulty in believing in the authenticity of respect offered by others.

Self-dislike and lack of a sense of worthiness may continue through much of life. While individuals can change toward self-acceptance and self-liking, it is difficult to accomplish this alone because of the self-perpetuating mechanism of self-dislike.

The Values of Self-Liking

However, before examining the ways in which such changes may be made, the values of self-acceptance and internal freedom bear review.

1. Accepting yourself as a unique and worthy being who, being human, is not immune from passions or behavior not approved by you.
2. Liking, valuing, respecting oneself and being unafraid to be oneself in varying situations. Seeking congruity between oneself and one's behavior. Being open with others and accepting openness from them by accepting their differences.
3. Allowing and encouraging others to have self-respect and to be themselves without coercion to be other than themselves.
4. Accepting others to be listened and responded to as worthy persons in their own right.
5. To be freed from destructive urges toward oneself or others and to have no need to punish others because of self-hurt or self-disapproval.
6. Valuing companionship on a deeply human basis that does not re-

quire diminution of self-respect or of integrity or demand it of others. Not needing companionship so desperately that one pretends to be what one is not.

7. Separating behavior from the real self and accepting the ownership of emotions, to learn and grow from knowing the causes of behavior and emotions, because to know is to lack fear and feel free.

8. Accepting reactions from others as useful if relevant to one's integrity and not merely to please others.

9. Using conflict and differences to generate further learning and growth, rather than as cause for ego defense.

10. Gaining a sense of well-being and fulfillment from the well-being of others.

11. Being open to gain and use both internal and external information about oneself.

12. Having internal strength sufficient to experience tranquility rather than tension. Having internal strength and sufficient self-understanding to welcome external approval when authentic and to recognize external approval that is not authentic.

Self-liking, self-esteem, self-respect and self-worthiness, if authentic, set the individual free to enjoy self and others. Being free internally releases the person from continuing hate and hostility toward self and others. Being oneself with others, unless used to laud oneself and disparage others, is responded to favorably and helps to release and free others. Being oneself with others is the basis of a deep companionship that helps each partner grow. Like the butterfly and the flower, open and noncoercive companionship rewards both.

So it is that self-liking marital partners have the confidence to review their relations without fear of hurt of rejection. Having the self-esteem and internal strength to undergo such a review provides information and stimulation from each partner to aid each in his growth. Individual self-liking and collaborative marriage review renews the marriage and aids in the growth of each.

Gaining Self-Awareness

The following model may help to illustrate how little most of us know about ourselves—and why—and how individuals can, usually with help from others, come to know more about themselves. The more a person knows about the motives that activate his responses and behavior, the more aware of causes of emotional reactions, the more knowledge of the consequences of any behavior, the greater is the understanding of oneself and the greater degree of self-acceptance.

Self-hate increases with self-ignorance. Understanding of others is strengthened by self-understanding.

As the model illustrates, there is much that individuals do not know about their motives and behavior. The less they know the more they prevent themselves from discovering about themselves.

The Johart Window[1]

	Known to self	Not Known to Self
Known to Others	Public Open	Blind
Not Known by Others	Hidden	Unconscious

The first window—known to oneself and known by others—represents knowledge all have about the individual. The individual knows his or her own height, color of hair, outer garments worn, and knows others have the same information. This public, open area includes information about general appearance, occupation, home, etc. In terms of the *total knowledge* that could be known about an individual it is relatively small. Many persons keep this area small for fear that further knowledge about themselves could be used to damage them. Persons differ in the extent to which they remain closed about themselves.

The second window—representing the knowledge the individual has about himself but is carefully not revealed to others—is the hidden area. Obviously no person would reveal all about himself, but this area is overly large for most individuals. The area comprises self-knowledge about feelings and emotions toward self and others that persons have been taught are bad or weak, motives they would not want others to know about, behaviors about which they feel guilty (often needlessly), actions they fear antagonize others, thoughts they worry others might disapprove. This vast array of self-

[1] J. Luft, *Group Process—An Introduction to Group Dynamics* (Palo Alto, Ca.: Mayfield Publ. Co., formerly National Press: 1970). Used with permission of the author.

knowledge hidden from others includes what the individual does not like about himself and feels guilty about, as well as thoughts and information others might not be interested in hearing. For many, the part that is disliked about the self is assumed to be disliked by others—a feeling which may or may not be true. The individual has few ways of knowing. Responses from others, if forthcoming, may be misread or distorted in hearing.

The hidden area is one full of insecurities and unresolved doubts—social, physical, occupational—that help to bring about self-rejection. Often, as a result, a variety of behaviors are used to prop up the tottering ego—boasting, braggadocio, name-dropping, tough behavior. One executive reported that for many years he tried to present a calm, hard, decisive front while inside he quaked with fear that others would discover how weak he really felt.

It is clear that in any social interaction there is always much that is unsaid and hidden. The question is whether too much is hidden preventing an open, sharing, noncontrolling relationship.

The third window—the blind area—represents the knowledge and perceptions others have about the individual that is neither known by the person nor does he realize others know. Persons communicate many messages in many ways—choice of words, inflection of voice, emotional intensity, posture, facial expression, muscular tension. From this multiplicity of messages others make assumptions or judgments, often incorrect, about the motivations, beliefs, thoughts and feelings of the other. The individual does not realize all the messages he sends out or which ones were received, and he or she is seldom told. All the individual can do is make interpretations of the responses received. Some are complete silence, polite but vague statements or smiling agreements. The original individual, in turn, makes judgments about the responses. So sender and receiver hear and react to partial information.

If fewer thoughts were hidden and more information were communicated, individuals would have fewer blind areas and relate to others in less darkness.

Recently Martha was playing golf in a foursome with some women friends. She had just received some distressing news about a health problem of another dear friend, but she didn't want to say anything in the foursome for fear of disturbing the others' game. The news did disturb Martha's usual play. After a few holes of play, one woman said to Martha, "I realize something must be bothering you, and I'm very sorry." She didn't inquire further, but was gently supportive of Martha throughout the rest of the game.

Late in the game when it no longer would disturb the group, Martha told her news to the other women, knowing they would hear about it later anyway. Later, after she returned home, she thought again about the extreme sensitivity of the one woman, her forebearance in not making inquiries and her tenderness to Martha during the rest of the day. Feeling that she would like to be told in a similar situation, she called the woman to tell her how sensitive and understanding she had been and how much she, Martha, deeply appreciated it. The other lady said she felt overwhelmed because no one before had ever told her she was sensitive and understanding of others. She said Martha's call made her day and helped her to feel good about herself.

Being open with one's feelings and reactions helps to create openness in others. It seems one of the tragedies of human relations is that persons are uncertain about giving information helpful to another lest they be misunderstood. It takes security and self-liking not to fear being open with others.

Unfortunately, the knowledge in the blind area known to others but not to oneself may have a profound influence on motives of which the individual is unaware. Feedback from others, even if momentarily painful, may help an individual become aware of behavior and motives not desired and which could be changed.

An individual whose sad facial expression and drooping shoulders made him appear to others as forlorn, helpless and lost, was in his abilities anything but lost and helpless. But over the years, without being aware of what he was doing, he had not only allowed, but used, his appearance to gain support and help from others.

In a learning group concerned with self-awareness and human relations, he gained feedback as to how others perceived him, different from the way he perceived himself. More importantly, he learned that for years he had been using his appearance to manipulate others. He was shocked, but helped by the information. While obviously unable to change this aspect of his appearance, once he recognized his motivation he was able to show more strength and confidence in his appearance and to be less manipulative.

One very obvious reason why feedback is seldom given is that there is a lack of knowledge as to how it will be received. If it has any negative aspect, it can be denied and an enemy made. If highly rewarding, it may be heard as insincere flattery. To stress again, as one is open about oneself there is a tendency for others to become more open.

Those who are most frightened, most hidden, and most defensive are usually those who most desperately need the information about their blind areas, but are most likely neither to accept nor receive it. Others quickly recognize how open and willing an individual is to receive reactions about his behavior.

In many training groups in human behavior, we have noticed individuals during the first difficult hours sit with fists clenched and perspiration dotting their foreheads and angrily deny they are feeling tension.

The hidden and blind areas described have an extremely important impact on each of us. Anyone who is overly hidden and defensive seldom has feedback given to him, except, perhaps, when another has become overly irritated and speaks from his anger. Thus, the more hidden and covered the person, the less knowledge usually gained about blind areas of behavior and suspected motives. With no input of knowledge about himself coming to the individual, there is no force to bring about change.

Conversely, if the individual is able to receive, accept without defensiveness, and utilize applicable information about himself lying in the blind area, there is an increase in self-awareness. Known information is usually far more innocuous than one feared. Knowing now what others already know, there is less to hide. Willingness to learn about areas unknown to oneself increases the willingness of others to feed back helpful information. Again, open persons encourage openness in others. So the process of decreasing defensiveness and hiding efforts decrease blind areas and increase self-awareness.

The last window in the model represents the unconscious—the area of unknown motivation that even deep therapy will not entirely bring to the level of consciousness. However, this window also includes a subarea known as the preconscious. This is a layer of knowledge not present on the awareness level but capable of being recalled if resistance is not too great.

How Does an Individual Go About Gaining Greater Self-Knowledge and Discovery of Blind Areas?

Self-awareness, self-liking and respect for the basic integrity of others is, as has been written before, vital to an effective renewal of the marriage and the stimulating, supportive companionship needed for a successful retirement. A couple with encrusted patterns of inadequate or punishing communication developed over many years, with individual characteristics of insecurity, self-doubt or self-disliking or with no previous attempt at a calm, collaborative examination of their relationships might find a sudden review of their marriage filled with recriminations.

Ideally development of greater self-awareness should begin long before retirement. Ideally marital reviews held periodically, if successful in renewing the marriage, would provide experience for the crucial review at retirement. As a result each partner grows in a sense of self-worthiness.

But any couple, irrespective of past experience, can use their planning for retirement or their adjustment at retirement together to look at their relationships, sweep out the debris of past incidents, hurts and misunderstandings, and endeavor to develop the kind of relationships suited to their closer living and to the enjoyment of their years of retirement. A thoughtful, calm, collaborative, honest and nonfearful look at what they want these precious years to be like and what each individual will need to do to make these years pleasant can occur. Out of such a searching may come, if each partner can level with and accept help from the other, the elimination of some of the blind areas each has been unaware of over the years. The result would be greater self-understanding and increased ease with oneself.

But self-awareness, the reduction of blind areas and the true acceptance of oneself does not come effortlessly nor usually without assistance from others. This assistance is not easy to secure. Rationalization of one's motives and behavior leads all too readily to defensiveness if comments contrary to one's rationalizations are made by others.

Asking friends or strangers out of the blue to give feedback about one's behavior is seldom successful. If given, the recipient might reject the information as distorted or falsely motivated, and not at all what the individual wishes to hear. The person being asked does not know the purpose one had in asking or what will be done with the information. Is the purpose to be reassured? Would friendship be lost and enmity gained if the knowledge were viewed as negative?

Self-introspection *without adequate training* may prove equally useless. Asking oneself about one's motives can lead to vindications rather than learning real motives. Meditation *without proper training* can easily result in greater self-dislike as data from others which could diminish self-dislike are blocked out.

What individuals not seeking deep therapy can find of benefit in increasing their self-awareness is to utilize a human, responding mirror reflecting back aspects of the person blind to self, and providing information about the consequences of one's behavior and appearance upon others. To paraphrase Robert Bruce's famous poem, each person needs a way of seeing oneself the way others do. With such information blind areas could become fewer, motives more correctly understood, and with greater self-understanding, increased self-acceptance would generally follow.

The simplest example of helpful feedback carefully given may be the following. Leland was having trouble with his approaches to the green on that particular golfing day. A playing companion said nothing for a few holes. Then he spoke: "Watching you, I notice you are keeping your weight on the right side. Perhaps that's why your approaches fall short. Do you think it would help to shift a little more weight to your left leg?"

But such a mirror is difficult to secure and accept. Before the person can receive reflections and information about himself as true, there must be trust. Trust must include belief that the feedback is sincerely intended to be helpful, is not distorted, is sensitive to how much information the person can take in without defensiveness or hurt at that period of self-awareness, and provides the individual with information he can use for change or improvement. To receive information from such a mirror about aspects of the person about which nothing can be done is hurtful, destructive knowledge.

A human, responding, nonpunitive mirror is a fragile human relationship. If feedback from such a mirror, composed of one or more persons, is immediately rejected and not even momentarily considered, its usefulness is lost. For a human mirror to increase in usefulness, information reflected or reported should be carefully heard, thoughtfully considered, and used if applicable.

To be specific, if the human mirror is one's spouse, trust must be present that the feedback is clearly helpfully motivated, sensitive to the feelings of the person involved, and not impelled by personal needs to control, make the other over, or prove superiority.

The use of small groups to serve as human mirrors for members has come into wide acceptance over the past thirty years. The original T-Group (T for training in human relations, sensitivity and self-awareness) was pioneered by the National Training Laboratories in 1947 in Bethel, Maine.[2]

Training groups are conducted for short, intensive periods ranging from a few days through two weeks. Some programs are conducted on a once or twice a week basis as part of a university program. Schools, churches, industries, private training organizations and other institutions and organizations carry such programs, typically open to the average person. Few communities of medium or large size would fail to have some such program. Inquiries to local junior or community colleges or to a university or a church would indicate where such programs are held and how qualitatively sound they are.

In most groups providing a human mirror for the development of greater sensitivity and self-awareness of the members, time is spent in forming a group that makes each member feel he is identified as unique and is respected, listened to and expected to participate. Shaping this kind of group is difficult as usually the collection of individuals has no formal leadership, though it does have the assistance of a trained facilitator or a trainer. Through such a struggle to create such conditions, trust builds so that members can receive feedback from others with lessened defensiveness. The trusted mirror then provides information each member can use in reducing

---

[2]Those interested in the theory, method and application of the T-Group see: L. P. Bradford, J. R. Gibb, and K. D. Benne, *T-Group Theory and Laboratory Method* (New York: Wiley, 1964) (this has been considered the classic work on this subject); E. Schein and W. Bennis, *Personal and Organizational Change Through Group Methods* (New York: Wiley, 1965); R. Golenbiewski and A. Blumberg, *Sensitivity Training and the Laboratory Approach* (Itasca, Ill.: Peacock, 1970); Carl Rogers, *Carl Rogers on Encounter Groups* (New York: Harper, Row, 1970); J. R. Gibb, *Trust* (Los Angeles: Guild of Tutors Press, 1978).

blind areas, becoming more aware of motives and gaining more understanding of himself and others.

Even the process of creating a group from a collection of individuals furnishes information about how behavior is perceived by others. So, through the creation of learning groups and by other methods, trust is developed to a point that a human, responsive and responding mirror aids individuals in self-understanding so necessary for self-acceptance, for freedom in internal feeling and for more open, honest, respecting relations with others. Experience in such a group could do much to make marital reviews and renewals more effective. In fact, the basic elements of trust and non-punitive, non-destructive feedback are essential both to such training groups and to marital relations.

In all such training groups that we have been involved in or conducted, most of the participants became more aware of their own feelings, motives and behavior, and more sensitive to the needs and motives of others. Many were shocked by how little they knew and feared about themselves. It was comforting to know that many others in the group had the same experience.

In one such training situation, separate groups were held for husbands and wives. After a full day, when a husband and wife had retired to their bedroom, they would share with each other the events of the day each had experienced and what had been learned. They found this late-at-night marital group provided a tremendous opportunity to know each other more fully and to come closer together in sharing thoughts and feelings.

One couple, a year later, told us that whenever they felt out of communication or had differences that could mount into hurt and defensiveness, they would pause and hold their own T-Group to find the causes of their difficulty. Having learned to "level" with each other, they could now approach their problem as one to be solved, rather than as a situation causing continued recriminations and widening of the gulf in their communications. Here was obviously the beginning of periodic marriage reviews. But it took the learning in self-awareness each had gained in the formal groups.

It is difficult to comprehend how such a T-Group, or similar group under another name, can provide such learning for its members. Let us pretend we are attending such a self-awareness training group and see what actually happens.

Comparisons between the occurrences in a T-Group and what happens in many marriage situations are many and informative. From time to time, as we watch the T-Group develop, some comparisons will be made. Obviously, there are others that could be made.

The Training Program in Human Relations

You had decided to participate in this week-long program held at a training center some distance from your home. You understood that the program would be so full that it would necessitate your staying at the center for the entire period.

It is now Sunday evening. Late this afternoon you attended a short opening session in which more than a hundred men and women were gathered. You knew no one and it seemed that practically everyone was a stranger to the rest. You learned at this session that you, like others, would be in a small group for nearly eight hours each day and evening for the rest of the week. Although you heard words of explanation, you really didn't comprehend what would happen in the groups.

It is nearly eight o'clock, the designated hour, and so you enter the small room to which your group has been assigned. You see a circle of eleven chairs, some of which are already occupied. You sit down and rather awkwardly say hello to those already present. Individuals are sitting silently and you feel an atmosphere of stiffness and tension. The person next to you hands you a crayon and a piece of cardboard folded like a tent. You notice others have printed their first names or nicknames on their cards and placed them on the floor so others can read the names. You write your nickname on the card, place it in front of you, and then look around at the other cards trying to connect names to faces as quickly as you can.

Shortly the eleven chairs are occupied, and one person, whom you recall was introduced as one of the trainers at the opening session, breaks the silence. He reminds all that they will be together for much of the time each day during the week, that he assumes they wish to learn more about human relations and themselves, that he believes that if they discuss what happens and why as they form a group and work together, each can learn a great deal. He then says that he doesn't intend to be the leader, but will endeavor to be helpful, as he assumes others will, when it seems appropriate. Then he stops.

There is silence (it seems to you to last forever), so thick it feels suffocating. One person, rather timidly, says she is unclear about what the trainer had meant, so the trainer merely repeats what he had said, adding nothing. Again a silence. Finally one person (you notice the card in front of his chair indicates his name is Bill) breaks the silence by saying it was usually customary in strange groups for persons to introduce themselves so everyone can know who they are. Bill suggests they do so. A man named Stu quickly says, "That's a good idea. Bill, why don't you start?"

Mary asks the trainer if it is all right to do this. (You think it is wise to find out if this is what the trainer wants.)

The trainer replies that such a decision is up to the group. (You feel let down by the answer. Is every decision to be made by the group without the leader's approval? Will chaos prevail?)

The trainer sees his answer as crucial at this point. If he answers the dependency request by giving or withholding approval, he will create more dependency on him and make it harder for the members to learn and the group to develop through tackling its own problems.

A marriage is an organization like a group. If one partner must make all the decisions or give approval before the other can act, dependency is created and growth inhibited. Support can be given by one partner to the other as the trainer does, by indicating belief the other also has the competency to make decisions.

Without further ado, Bill introduces himself by giving his full name, title, organization and scope of his activities. (It sounds prestigious.) He then turns to the individual on his right who makes a similar introduction. After three more persons have introduced themselves, essentially giving only "name, rank and serial number," it becomes the trainer's turn.

He says, "Before talking about myself, I have some questions to ask the group members, and I would like to share some reactions I have about the previous introductions. First, I wondered why there was no group decision to have introductions. As I recall the sequence of events, Bill suggested introductions and Stu agreed. Mary then asked if I approved. I thought I said the decision was up to the group. No one said anything, and Bill went ahead to introduce himself, perhaps taking permission from Stu. I guess I have three questions. Did

Bill take Stu's agreement as a group approval? Or was there some nonverbal signal from the group that told Bill to go ahead? Or did Bill go ahead without checking with the group?

Bill speaks up quickly to say that because no one had objected he thought his suggestion was helping the group get started. "After all," he says, "silence means consent."

In many marital situations, a wife's silence signals acquiescence and so reinforces the husband's pattern of making unilateral decisions. But the silence may cover resentment, hostility and the demeaning acceptance of an inferior role.

Joe, another member, says, "I don't believe that silence necessarily means consent. Our names are in front of us and I was considering whether I wanted to know anything more about people right now. I was a little afraid that knowing where people came from and what they did might prejudice me."

But Sally says, "I felt relieved when Bill started. I couldn't stand the awful silence any longer."

Some other persons indicate they were in favor of the introductions or for anything that would get them started.

The trainer reflects that while the individual tension was too high for the group to make a total group decision, the idea that the group should make decisions about what it does, rather than permitting one or two persons to do so, was now out in the open.

In many marriage situations unilateral decisions made by one partner tend to weaken the ability of the other and to create an unbalanced marriage. Wives have reported they found it futile to fight their husbands and so submitted to decisions of which they had no part. When they became widows they felt lost.

The trainer continues to share his reactions to the previous introductions. He says, "I've learned a little about the positions and organizations those who have introduced themselves hold and belong to, but I don't feel I have learned much about them as persons that will help me relate to them in this group. I guess I have been introduced to organizations rather than persons, and, personally, I would rather know about them as individuals. How do the rest of you feel? What do you think we need to know about each other so that we can become a good group for the rest of the week we are together?"

The trainer stops to see if there are any reactions. (You feel jolted because you had accepted introductions as a normal procedure without thinking about the consequences. Besides, you were feeling anxious as to how people would react to your introduction. What status would you have in this group?)

Bill jumps in to say he thought the introductions were important because they made it possible to "place" people. The trainer asks if it was necessary to "place" people particularly by what they did outside the group? Was the group going to develop a "pecking order" or hierarchy of those who were more important and those less? Would this create a group where everyone felt accepted?

Stereotypes get in the way of close, sharing, openly communicative relationships, whether in marriage or any other situation. Seeing the marital partner merely as a wife and woman, or a husband and man, rather than as a person, could cut off important information about the feelings of the other. Often stereotypic labelings result in put-downs: "You don't know what you're talking about," and, "This is a problem for men."

Thelma, who has been quiet up to the present, remarks she was feeling more and more anxious as the introductions proceeded. She was "just" a housewife serving as a volunteer in a community organization, and now she was afraid she would not be accepted in the group because she didn't have any prestigious title. Several persons hurry to reassure her. Bill, who had wanted to "place" people, says he didn't mean to exclude anyone. He just feels more comfortable knowing what people do for a living.

With no more discussion, the trainer speaks briefly about himself, describing his interests, talking about the things he enjoys in himself, as well as the areas where he wants to grow, and mentions his family and the ways in which they are important to him.

The trainer knows that most individuals avoid revealing much about themselves in a strange situation. He also is aware that people both seek and react to status in others. He hopes his intervention will help those in the group to begin to see each other as persons rather than as "executive," "teacher," "volunteer." Only then can trust, rather than fear of rejection, develop. With trust they will be able to share feelings and experiences freely instead of reacting to power.

There are a number of analogies between the group struggle over introductions and the development of an openly effective and sharing marriage. Often couples live side by side for years without knowing much about the internal thoughts and feelings of each other. Power and dominance-submission relationships are common in marriages. In many instances the dominance of one leads to the submission of the other, resulting in false, unhealthy relationhips. The submissive one tends not to exist as a whole person in the eyes of the other, but rather as an extension or projection of the other. Submission does not produce a sense of self-worth. Just as the members of the group needed to become aware that their pattern of introduction might lead them to a hierarchy of power and powerlessness, dominance and submission, so can marital partners become aware of their own stereotypes of each other and whether their relationship demands submission of one to the other, with all the consequences of unshared and unrevealed feelings and inhibited growth.

Introductions, following the trainer's, combine more information about the persons, why they came to the program, what they hope will happen, personal concerns and interests, family. In addition individuals give briefer, less status-seeking information about work and organization. At the end of the introductions there is a rather lengthy discussion about the purpose—and possible dangers—of introductions in a group such as this. They begin to see that if they are to learn from their relationships together, their relations must be based on their identifications as persons, not as symbols of power and authority brought in from the outside. One individual comments that he likes the idea of the group spending the week in the "here and now" with as little intrusion from the outside as possible. He adds that he is fascinated by the idea of spending an entire week on the group's relationships. Others have doubts. But most agree that they feel more relaxed now than they did at the beginning of the evening.

The trainer thinks to himself that marital partners would increase their understanding of each other and the sharing of thoughts if each really viewed the other as a unique and interesting person rather than as a role symbol.

You are puzzled as you go to your room after the meeting. Really not much has happened. Eleven persons have introduced themselves. Not a great deal in terms of meetings you customarily attend where motions are made and decisions quickly reached. You have much to think about. Individuals in the group have already come sharply into focus, more distinctly than in most meetings where your attention has been on the subject and not on the individual—certainly not in the same way. You begin to think about every person in the group, and you are fascinated by a new way of looking at people—not as objects out there who might or might not be troublesome or helpful, but as different, unique human beings like yourself who will relate to you in various ways. What interesting and significant abilities might lie within various persons! This could be an adventure in discovering people.

What might all this mean to the usual groups and meetings you attend? Would a better understanding of the feelings of the members and what was really happening in the group make a great difference in its effectiveness? Or would it take too much time? How could you ever get others to see what you are beginning to see? You will have to think about all this.

This leads you to think about Bill. How was he feeling now? Had he learned anything from the evening's experience or did he still believe he was right? Thelma's statement about only being a housewife, plus Bill's anxiety as to how he would be received, show how easy it is to create a pecking order, making those at the bottom feel unhappy and unwanted. You look forward to the next meeting. It is difficult falling asleep with so many thoughts racing through your mind.

The trainer wonders whether Bill is like many husbands who feel they must always be right.

When the group meets again the members wait for the trainer to start the session. He sits in silence, also waiting, until the members realize that he really isn't going to lead the sessions. Silence prevails for some minutes. Finally Bill opens the discussion again. He remarks that the group has to do something. Everyone can't sit silently for a week. He presents a topic for discussion, one having nothing to do with the purpose of the course or the previous evening. At least, he says, they can share opinions and maybe they can learn something that way. Obviously, the trainer isn't going to help them.

The trainer realizes that Bill's cheap shot at him was a measure of Bill's anxiety. How many cheap shots in marriage, the trainer speculates, grow out of insecurity and anxiety?

Joe, who had disagreed with Bill's statement the night before that "silence means consent," now says in a very decisive and commanding voice that he doesn't like Bill's suggested topic. He suggests the group talk about their problems of leadership back home. Sally comments she thought the group was supposed to work on how to make their group effective, but her point is drowned out by Bill who loudly defends his original topic, giving a series of logical reasons why it should be adopted. Several members try to break in but Joe's voice overrides everyone else's as he argues for his topic. Bill and Joe are now talking at each other, ignoring the other group members. Attempts by others to intercede are unsuccessful.

The trainer thinks about the many marital battles that are largely emotional but with little substance.

The trainer listens to the struggle for some time, waiting to see if any of the members will try to stop the argument between Bill and Joe and bring the discussion back to the group. At a brief pause in the argument, he finally speaks. Bill and Joe stop to listen because they are not certain what power and authority the trainer will wield. The trainer says, "I've been aware as Bill and Joe talked at each other that individuals sat back as if they weren't part of the group. What is happening? How do the rest of you feel?"

Bill speaks up to say that anyone could have spoken up if they had wanted to. He and Joe were just trying to get the group rolling.

Bob says, "As far as I'm concerned, that isn't correct. Bill and Joe have strong, commanding voices. I tried to say something a number of times but neither Bill nor Joe bothered to listen. So I quit."

You feel the same way. You wonder if the entire week is going to be dominated by Bill and Joe.

Mary remarks, "They were like two bulls fighting for leadership and I didn't see what I could do."

Bill vehemently denies he was trying to be the leader or to run the group. He was just trying to help the group. Mike comments that it isn't a very good way to help by cutting everyone else out of the conversation.

Joe ruefully admits he was fighting Bill. At first he thought he was trying to protect the group from Bill's dominance, but he guesses he has to admit that he had been trying hard since the beginning of the previous evening to get the leadership for himself. You ask him if he had heard others trying to join the debate. Joe admits he didn't listen to anyone but Bill. It wasn't that he was so stuck on his idea as he was determined to beat Bill. He says, "I guess neither Bill nor I listened to anybody else. Maybe we didn't even listen to each other."

Joe continues, "I think I realized something out of all this. I'm not sure I like what I think I've learned, but I think I've dominated or tried to dominate every group I've been in back home. Maybe that's why I've had trouble with others."

The trainer speaks slowly and clearly. "Joe, I suspect you really feel very good about what you learned about yourself. I believe you also feel equally good in being willing to be so open in sharing this learning with all of us. I don't know how others feel, but I believe I have come to know Joe better as a person now. I also think you just helped the group more than you realize. How do others feel?"

A number of members nod their heads. Roger, who has said very little thus far in the meetings, now speaks up. "I thought Joe's admission took a lot of courage and it certainly helped me. Before Joe told us about how he has acted before coming here, I would have been afraid to mention anything wrong in my behavior. Now I feel freer and more relaxed because no one seemed disturbed over Joe's admission or thought less of him. I feel we are more relaxed now."

Bill still seems to feel the need to justify himself. He says he, for one, has not been fighting for leadership. Before he can continue, Mike cuts in to say, "Bill, you're just being defensive now. Listen to the rest of us." Bill subsides.

The trainer has two thoughts. He wonders if in making Joe's insight and courage stand out he has punished Bill and helped him to be more defensive. He hopes not. Second, he thinks of the husbands and wives who reject without consideration the kind of feedback both Joe and Bill received.

Stu turns to the trainer. "I'm sorry," he says, "that you interrupted their fight. I knew they were struggling for leadership, and I was wondering how it was going to end."

The trainer responds, "Thanks, Stu, for your willingness to tell me how you felt. Perhaps I was premature in not waiting longer to see what would happen."

The trainer hopes that his response will serve as a model for members in being open in giving and accepting feedback. He has thanked Stu for his help and his willingness to tell how he felt. He has accepted the feedback, but without necessarily using it—a decision belonging to the individual—by saying "perhaps" he had been premature. He has not been defensive or rejected Stu's comment.

But several others say they felt relieved the fight had been stopped. They had been uncomfortable but didn't know what to do. The trainer asks why they hadn't tried to bring the leadership struggle out on the floor. They answer that they didn't know whether it was the trainer's responsibility to stop the fight. They weren't sure of the ground rules.

This begins a lively and serious discussion lasting for the rest of the morning about group ground rules, member behavior, feedback and trust.

The trainer considers what he should do—and how he should proceed—in dealing with the episode of the conflict for leadership between Bill and Joe so that it would be most helpful for the learning of group members. It is clear that as long as the basic issue of leadership conflict is covered over with "logical" arguments on a surface topic, the real problem will remain on the hidden level and could be dealt with only with difficulty. (The trainer thinks of the many marital situations in which husband and wife fight interminably without ever reaching the basic hidden problem.) The leadership struggle will continue under different guises immobilizing the group.

The problem facing the trainer is what to do. If he merely stops the fight, even if this brought the struggle to the surface, he would only be placing his leadership above Bill and Joe, leaving the group in a dependency pattern to him. He hopes that by only reporting his feelings and observations as those of one person and then checking with group members for their reactions, and if his reporting is calm, factual and nonblaming, other members will give their reactions and by so doing solve a basic group problem. In addition they will begin to learn to give and receive feedback in a nonhostile way.

As it turns out, the trainer sees, members do report their reactions making it necessary for the two combatants to face, however defensively and reluctantly, their own motives. The trainer is tremendously pleased with the insights into himself that Joe gained and his willingness to share this learning with others. This is a distinct plus for the future learning of others. While Bill remains defensive on the surface, the trainer speculates that he may also have learned something about his behavior and motives. Time will tell. At all events, the conflict is out in the open and the members well prepared to handle it and other problems that might emerge. They are now better qualified to help each other.

As the morning discussion continues members become more and more convinced that the group really does belong to them. If anyone feels uncomfortable, or is aware of actions hurting the group, feelings and observations should be mentioned and other members checked to see how they feel and what they observe. Members see this responsibility as both a steering mechanism for the group and as a protection for other group members.

An implicit decision is reached that no member is to hog "air time" and that each member deserves being carefully listened to in order to have full participation.

Bob raises the question of group leadership. He says he had started out with the firm idea that every small group needed a strong, decisive leader and he had expected the trainer would carry out this function. When the trainer deliberately didn't serve as leader but confined himself to commenting on what he saw and felt, and inquired how others felt, he, Bob, was as lost as anyone. At first, he says, he welcomed Bill's efforts to lead the group as something that needed to be done. But when he saw the conflict develop between Bill and Joe, how it didn't get anywhere, and how he felt when he couldn't make himself heard, he began to think of leadership in a different way. Essentially, he says now, he began to see leadership in two ways. First, when anyone said something that moved the group forward, rather than held it up, that person at that moment was serving a leadership function. For example, when Joe told what he had learned, he was more of a leader than when he fought Bill for leadership. Thelma helped the group to realize the dangers of two classes of membership when she said she was only a "volunteer." "If this were true," Bob continues thoughtfully, "everybody was a leader at some time in the group." Second, he says he is beginning to see a different role for the designated leader. It is to help and encourage all members to be responsible for the group progress. He wants to think about this for a while.

The trainer has a number of thoughts about Bob's statement. He is impressed that Bob had come close to the real essence of leadership. Second, he is aware how Bob's remarks had helped in the critically important validation or affirmation of the identity and worthiness of each member.

Bob's statement starts a long discussion of leadership that comes to no definite conclusion. The group can't quite differentiate between the role of a leader and leadership functions. Members feel that somehow a leader should emerge in their group. At the same time they are increasingly clear that everyone in the group should feel free to play an active part in the group. They aren't yet ready to solve the dilemma in their thoughts.

The trainer, who says nothing during this long period in which the group worked on the crucial and knotty problem, has thoughts he keeps to himself. He feels pleased the group had been able to tackle so difficult a problem so early. But he knows that to say he is pleased would be to reassert leadership by rewarding the group. His second thought deals with the number of married couples in which one took leadership and the other submitted to that leadership with the issue never raised, nor their desires expressed.

Alice, who has said little thus far, suddenly changes the direction of the discussion. She says, "I wonder if we haven't been pretty brutal to each other. I've felt that some members have been deeply hurt by some things said to them. I don't think it is right to hurt people. Bill was told he was trying to control all of us when he may merely have been endeavoring to help. Mike called him defensive, which is not a very polite thing to say. Joe said he was fighting Bill's efforts to take over the group when maybe it was only Joe fighting, not Bill. I wonder if we haven't hurt Bill. He hasn't said much lately. I'm afraid we are just going to tear each other apart sadistically. I think we ought to be more careful."

Bill says gruffly that he hasn't been hurt. He is too strong for that. But he does agree with Alice. He certainly wouldn't like negative remarks made about the women in the group. That wouldn't be chivalrous. In fact, he doesn't like the idea of anyone being carved up.

Stu joins in and supports Alice and Bill. He thinks the group, and particularly the trainer, are going too far. This is not a couch session and none of them are psychiatrists, unless it is the trainer and then he should say so. Those who want to be mauled over can indicate their wishes and leave the rest alone.

The trainer thinks that the statements are highly emotionally charged and may result from personal anxiety. Furthermore, the remarks equate feedback as always negative, whereas there had occurred already instances of very positive feedback—praise to Joe for his courage and openness, to Thelma for raising the dual membership issue. However, the trainer is glad that the issue has been raised. Ground rules certainly need to be set that aid learning, prevent destructive results and are sensitive to the different defenses of individuals. He decides to wait and see what happens.

There is silence for a few moments while members individually consider whether group members have been hurt and whether all their faults and inadequacies are to be dragged out in the open for all to see. There is doubt and worry showing on faces.

Finally Joe speaks. "What Alice, Bill and Stu are saying is very serious. I don't think any of us here wishes to be torn apart. Certainly I don't. But we are here to learn. I've been thinking over what has happened so far, and I don't see that anyone has been hurt. I'm extremely grateful for what I learned about myself from your reactions when I tangled with Bill. I've gone all my life and not learned that. As I realized that our struggle kept you all out of the discussion, I couldn't help thinking how I got meetings to be very calm and peaceful because I managed to force people to agree with me by out-arguing or out-shouting them. I'm wondering now how they must have felt. Something I haven't mentioned—and it has been very hard for me even to think about—has been my relations with my wife. Not that our relations haven't been peaceful, but I realize now that I called the shots and she just submitted. What has she thought over these years? I can't wait to go home and talk with her. So I appreciate all I have learned, and I would hate to have any of you hold back in telling me things about my actions you observe."

There is a mixed chorus of reactions from others. Some are fearful of any reaction they might volunteer. Others say if they don't get some reactions to their behavior, how can they learn. That's why they came here.

The trainer asks the group if the members can resolve their dilemma by discussing ways in which members can be helped by each other without the efforts being destructive rather than beneficial. What ground rules are needed? How much trust is necessary so no one feels another is being maliciously attacked?

The last hour of the morning is spent, as a result of the trainer's questions, on the problem of helping each other and on learning. The group finally agrees that without information from others, an individual is unable to know the consequences of his behavior on others. At the same time, such information needs to be carefully given. The following points about helping, as the trainer notes them, are carefully discussed by the members.

1. Feedback of reactions differs radically from criticism. The object is not to make anyone feel guilty and unworthy, but to help the individual see how others react.
2. Feedback requires trust that no one is trying to hurt another person. This, in turn, calls for sensitivity as to how the other person is feeling.
3. Feedback is essentially the nonjudgmental offering of information that the recipient has about the behavior of the subject and does not imply that the subject had "bad" motives. The offering is given on the assumption that it is vital information the subject may be able to use.
4. Feedback should not be defensively rejected, but listened to and considered. The person receiving feedback is under no duress to accept the information, but does need to hear and carefully consider it.
5. Feedback should never be given punitively or patronizingly. It should be honest to be helpful. It can be positive as well as revealing error.

If marital partners could offer each other usable information about behavior that may be pleasing or irritating in a way that is neither critical nor nagging, producing hostility and conflict or agreement under duress, each could be more helpful to the other. The partner receiving such information can decide whether to use the reactions of the other, but without pressure. The information given can be seen as helpful because others aren't likely to give it.

You leave the three-hour morning session with your mind whirling. Fortunately there is free time until four o'clock, so you have the afternoon after lunch for thinking. The morning has been full and fascinating. You have seldom had three hours go by so rapidly. Nor-

mally, back on the job, an hour's meeting always ssemed interminable. You review the morning in your own mind. Looking back,
the struggle between Bill and Joe could have been disastrous. It
might have kept up under cover for the entire week. You think of
how smoothly the trainer had helped to turn the tide, first by reporting his observations that the other members, by their posture and
ultimate silence, had withdrawn from the group momentarily, and
second, by asking for reactions from the group. The trainer, as you
think about it, has not punished Bill and Joe, pulled leadership rank,
or even suggested that the struggle end. He had merely in a couple of
sentences said that he observed persons sitting back and wondered
what was happening and what others thought. There was the implication that the group could handle the situation once it was out in the
open. It was a lesson in leadership.

Then there was Joe's confession. Somehow his willingness to tell
the group what he had learned about himself changed the entire
atmosphere of the meeting. People seemed to relax. The two incidents caused the group to think about ground rules. Again, you remember, the trainer had asked one simple question, "Why didn't
people speak up when they saw something wrong?" That one question stimulated a good half hour's conversation. As you think about
it, the trainer had really spoken only about four times all morning.
But each statement of observation or question started a whole train
of thought.

Bob's thinking about the difference about leaders and leadership
really was great. You will have to think a lot about that. Really, Bob
proved his own point. His "out-loud" thinking really moved the
group at that moment, so Bob actually must have been the leader at
that moment.

Then came Alice's intervention. That certainly started a storm.
Really, it brought to the surface what had been in the back of
everyone's mind. An entire hour's excited discussion resulted.
Marvelous! You had never realized before how one important statement led so far and stimulated the next important idea. The way
ideas and problems flowed naturally was amazing. In most groups
you had known an agenda had to be set up and followed closely. Unless the leader stated the next agenda item and kept the meeting's attention on it, only desultory conversation resulted. Here there was no

stated agenda but the group went from one problem to another effortlessly and with no tight control. It was exciting to watch. You wonder if meetings back home could be run differently—not exactly like this one, but certainly with the freedom for everyone to contribute naturally and to feel part of the situation. It is certainly something to think about.

At four o'clock the group gathers again for a two-hour session. As usual, silence exists for a few moments, but now the silence seems more natural and members seem more relaxed as they wait to see who will begin. Surprisingly, it is Thelma. She speaks timidly and softly as if she isn't sure of her reception.

She says, "I feel hesitant to bring up my problem so early when I'm sure the rest of you have greater ones, but I came to this session to see if I could get any help on a personal problem that has been bothering me for years."

She stops to see the reaction of the group members. Someone says, "Go ahead."

So she continues. "You will recall that last night during the introductions I said I was just a housewife. That sort of sums up my problem. Every time I do something, it never seems to attract any notice from others. My mind tells me that being a housewife and mother can be a very important job in life, but I sense from the attitudes and tones of voice of those around me that I'm not very competent. I'm not sure I always felt this way, but in recent years I've felt more and more inadequate and incompetent and unworthy. I've got to a point where at times I hate myself, while at other times I feel I'm not as inadequate as people seem to think I am. That's why I took this volunteer job, but even there I'm at the bottom of volunteer work. I feel torn up inside by all this. I don't suppose anyone here can help me, but I had to make this last try."

While the trainer is impressed by her courage and her openness to feedback, he wants to see how the group will react to her request for help. Certainly, she has shown how deep is her emotion and anguish. Would the members hear this as such or embarrassedly try to brush her request away. He will see.

Stu is the first to respond. "Thelma, all you need is a dose of confidence, just say to yourself that you're all right and this problem will disappear."

Bill echoes Stu's advice and others rush in to reassure her that they think she is very competent.

Thelma says, "That's what my husband says, but I don't think he really understands how I feel, and I don't feel he actually hears how deeply I'm suffering. He hasn't helped me and I think I need more than reassurance."

Then Joe speaks, "I think we are being very indifferent and unfair to Thelma. We aren't helping her, as she said, and I wonder why we have made no effort. We're giving her a pat on the back as if she were a small girl, which may make her feel we don't care about her. We're not hearing her as a mature person seeking help on a serious problem. My guess is that it took a lot of courage for Thelma to tell us about her problem."

He continues, "I'm certainly no psychiatrist and I don't have any answer, but I have noticed some things about you, as I'm sure others have, that you may not realize yourself but which might have something to do with how you are feeling. Do you know that each time you have spoken in this group, you have said something derogatory about yourself, or apologized for even speaking? Maybe that's what people hear, and maybe they judge you on those statements."

The trainer sees Joe's statements as a sincere attempt to give feedback about observed behavior—something concrete—which, while it doesn't get at the root of the problem, still offers Thelma something real to take hold of. He feels this might be an appropriate place to model how further help could be given.

The trainer enters the discussion with a question for Thelma. "If Joe is correct in his observation and its possible meaning for you, the question I would like to ask is where you learned to run yourself down and apologize, even when you say you don't always feel that way inside?"

There is silence while Thelma ponders for a few moments. Then she says, "I never thought of that. Now that you ask, maybe I learned it from my mother. When I was a small girl she always told me I was 'all thumbs' when I did anything. That phrase, 'all thumbs' has remained in my mind all these years and maybe part of me expects to fail before I start."

The trainer moves in quickly after Joe's statement with words he chooses carefully for a number of reasons. First, while he has also made the same observations to himself, to say so to the group would be "being a leader rewarding a star member," bringing back the dependency issue. So he merely says, "If Joe's observations are correct." Second, he knows that while the feedback to Thelma of how her behavior in the present is perceived is helpful because it is concrete evidence, Thelma still needs to get at the cause of this behavior, if possible. That is why he asks Thelma where she had learned such behavior. Third, by asking this question, the trainer wants to prevent Thelma from feeling more guilty about being apologetic by turning her thoughts away from self-blame to outside forces—the persons or events from which she had learned to act as she did. Thelma's thoughtful recall of her childhood, he feels, might help her work through the problem.

Bob says, "I've also noticed Thelma's tendency to down-grade herself and be very apologetic. At the same time, her few comments have been right on the beam and have aided the group. So, I've seen this discrepancy. Maybe we could help Thelma, if she is willing, to remind her every time she starts to apologize or down-grade herself. That way she might learn to bring her message right out in the beginning. Perhaps then people would see her differently and she would realize her competency. She could stop saying, 'just a volunteer,' or 'just a housewife,' or 'all thumbs.'"

Thelma agrees that would help and that she is grateful for the reactions she has received. She has a lot to think about now, she adds, but she feels that maybe she is on the right track.

The trainer thinks that Thelma has gained some very important insights and that she now has a potential for change. She has become aware of a blind area of her actions and demeanor leading to others' perceptions destructive to her sense of self-worth. Such self-awareness is the first necessary step in any change she might make in her behavior and her own self-estimation.

While the trainer knows her problem is not solved so easily and quickly, he feels that three important steps have been taken to help her. In addition the other group members may have learned much about how to help others beyond mere reassurance. The three steps are:

1. *Joe's nonhostile feedback of Thelma's outside actions he had observed gave her knowledge she didn't have before. With this*

*knowledge she might be able to modify her behavior so as to pro-
duce different perceptions in others and ultimately in her own
feeling about herself.*
2. *The trainer's question as to where she had learned her behavior
turned her thoughts away from self-blame and self-dislike to a
better understanding of herself and the effects others were having
on her.*
3. *Bob's suggestion of ways the group could help reinforce a direction for change.*

*What Thelma does with all this information remains the final
test. If she were only looking for sympathy and had no desire to
change, this would be apparent as the days went by. Given her
statement that her husband didn't understand her problem, this experience might help her improve communications at home. (The
trainer notices during the latter part of the week that Thelma tries
to modify her behavior. She participates more and makes direct, con-
cise interventions without preliminary apologies and self-deroga-
tory statements. Once, when she slips back, a group member reminds her. She takes the reminder in good grace.)*

Short as the late afternoon session has been you feel it, like the
preceding ones, has been different and exceedingly productive. You
feel caught up in Thelma's problem because it makes you think of
your own problems and what you hope to gain from the week's training session. You feel you have learned a lot about real helping. A pat
on the back to someone seriously seeking help might make you feel
good but it doesn't help the other person. You are impressed with
the power of feedback caringly given when the person wishes it, and
when the feedback is of observed behavior that has occurred in front
of everyone. You think the way Thelma reacted certainly answered
the fear of feedback expressed during the morning. Thelma certainly
wasn't hurt and she didn't respond as if she were being "carved up."
But obviously, you saw there had to be trust and a lack of fear and
defensiveness for feedback to work. And it had to be honest.

The second evening session shows the results of the hard work the
group has engaged in during the past twenty-four hours. The evening
begins in a relaxed manner with jokes and desultory conversation. It
seems clear that closer group feeling has developed with more trust
among members. At the same time there is no strong desire to work
hard this evening. Members are emotionally drained.

Toward the end of the meeting one member comments that the question the trainer had asked Thelma about how she had learned to feel as she did struck him more forcibly than anything that had happened thus far. It had set him thinking as deeply as he could about himself and asking himself how and where he had learned to do some of the things he didn't particularly like about himself. Later, he adds, he would like to share some of his thoughts with the group.

It is on this note that the group members thoughtfully disband for the evening.

The trainer realized the need for a rest and for group members, alone or in pairs, to talk and think through what had happened and what they had learned. Outside of joining occasionally in the joking, he made no further interventions. Enough was enough for now. The trainer also thinks that in marriage, alone time may be needed by either or both partners to digest feedback.

The rest of the week has its ups and downs. Problems and struggles for power, attention and leadership arise from time to time in different forms. Members work hard on forming from the collection of strangers a caring, trusting, close-knit group. At each session some member comes forth, or presents through behavior, a problem for the group to work on. Gradually each person becomes a part of the group through more open participation and sharing of personal thoughts and concerns. Hence, each member receives a kind of validation or affirmation of his identity. Problems individuals worry about often seem less drastic in the open light of group discussion. Each member has something different to learn, and most learn from the experience of others to be more self-accepting and more self-aware. As individuals find that trust can be created and that openness does not bring rejection, but instead help, they construct the human responding mirror so important in helping individuals learn and improve.

Such a training program in self-awareness and in skill in creating interpersonal relations helpful to self and others is, as has been said before, one way that persons can learn how to create a self-renewing marriage aiding each partner to greater self-understanding and to fuller communications.

The characteristics of a healthy, mutually fulfilling marriage providing equal autonomy, respect and opportunities for growth for both partners are complex and interlocking. The ways of developing and maintaining these characteristics are not easily achieved. They require joint efforts and patience.

1. The way in which a marriage handles crises and interpersonal problems is all-important. The resolution of differences and conflicts needs to occur at the time, rather than to be allowed to grow into cancerous hurts and hostilities.
2. The relationship between the partners is the responsibility of both. Therefore, neither should "blame" the other in a conflict while righteously remaining aloof from responsibility. The basic question of "What have I done to cause or encourage you to—" should always be asked.
3. Voicing reactions to certain behavior of the other partner differs vitally from voicing reactions against the person. Not, "You are a——," but, "Your behavior makes me react——. What do I do to cause such behavior?" If this issue is clear, behavior can be modified. But if the person and the behavior are assumed to be the same, only attack and defense result.
4. In any communication, feelings and reactions are as important and as concrete as "objective" facts.
5. Feedback of feelings and reactions help to provide a mirror for both partners.

The observations cited above help to create trust, freedom from rejection and increased openness of communication. The result is a mutually rewarding and fulfilling marriage.

While training in self-awareness and human relationships can usually help an individual or a couple to prepare for the emotional problems and adjustments in relationships often facing individuals and couples at retirement, there is much any individual or couple can do without such previous training.

Chapter 3 ended with a series of questions a husband and wife could ask themselves in renewing and re-energizing their marriage. Following is a list of self-searching questions any individual, or each partner, can ask. As these questions are answered thoughtfully and honestly, increased self-awareness may result.

1. What do I particularly like about myself? What do I dislike about myself? Can I accept myself and feel good about myself or do I live with constant self-dislike and guilt? Do I feel the need to be defensive about myself at all times? Under what conditions?
2. What are the parts of myself I feel I have neglected? Are they areas in which I feel I can still grow? Am I willing to make the ef-

fort? Can I accept help from others? Or do I believe it would be a
blow to my self-esteem to do so?

3. Do I find it difficult to admit error? Must I always prove myself
right? Am I afraid people will think less of me if I make a mis-
take? Can I laugh at myself?

4. Am I afraid of what other people will object to in me? What am I
hiding? What will it take to make me feel relaxed and unworried?

5. What makes me most anxious? How do I handle my anxieties?

6. Do I still feel I am in the rat-race? What must I do to find peace
and serentiy within myself?

7. What really makes me angry? What triggers the anger? Why that?
When and how did I learn to get angry at these events? Does anger
make me feel emotionally released or very guilty? Am I afraid to
get angry? What do I do with my anger? Bury it? Explode? Release it?

8. What emotions within me frighten me and create turmoil inside
me?

9. What do I feel most guilty about in myself? Why do I hold this
guilt? Where did I learn it? Does it make sense?

10. What stereotypes and judgments about others do I hold? Do I try
changing my attitudes and prejudices?

11. Do I make a serious effort to understand others or do I judge
them quickly?

12. What hostilities do I harbor against my spouse?

13. What are my basic conflicts? What internal difficulties do they
cause me?

14. In what way would I really like to change? Is there any change I
will try?

Chapter 5

Creating a Fulfilling Companionship

At retirement husband and wife come face to face unlike any other time in their lives. Position ended, children raised and family supported, one basic purpose in marriage has terminated. Now another important purpose remains to be discovered. This purpose is the development of a deeper, more sharing companionship that helps each partner cope with the many emotional and other problems commonly occurring in retirement. That companionship must replace losses in life structures caused by retirement, and energize each partner toward increased self-understanding, continued growth and vibrancy in living. Of necessity, the development of such a companionship should have built into it a process of continuous renewal and improvement of the companionship itself.

The alternative to the development of this fuller companionship is the continuation, now under new circumstances, of marital relations as they all too commonly have been—incomplete and ineffective communications, lack of understanding, hurts, hostilities, conflicts, unsolved interpersonal problems. By the time of retirement there is parallel living with passive acceptance by each partner of unliked and irritating behaviors of the other. But there is not a richly sharing companionship.

But a couple can generate or regenerate a companionship that is open, sharing, nonpunitive, nondemanding, nonsmothering, supportive and caring. The key words are *generation* and *regeneration* requiring desire and effort by both partners. Two individuals, largely separated and deeply occupied over the years by job and family functions, sex stereotypes and social expectations, all combining to produce a gulf between *male* and *female*, may now come together as two *persons*, freed from many of the forces dividing them before. Such a regenerated companionship makes retirement a time of renewal of life—not an ending.

A full companionship, in the context of this book, means that both partners desire and feel free to discuss openly and helpfully with each other problems, feelings, experiences and thoughts without punitiveness, hostility, devious and controlling motives or fear of conflict. The purpose of such discussion is to solve problems equitably, share inner thoughts and feelings, achieve stimulation, support and assistance. For such free and open discussion to occur, there must be self-honesty, as well as honesty to the other partner, internal strength to receive criticism without defensiveness and help without rejection, personal security and self-acceptance upon the part of both. Efforts to prove oneself right at the cost of proving the other wrong prevent the development of a full companionship. In short, such a companionship is built upon trust in the integrity, caring and openness of each. The ability to "level" with each other without abuse is a sign that trust is present.

A full companionship can provide many values, particularly at retirement time. Individuals have needs to gain and maintain a sense of self-worth, of special personhood, of respected individuality if they are to be emotionally healthy. They need to perceive and be perceived as having the ability to be self-determining. Their sense of self-worth should be sufficient for self-liking, instead of the self-dislike many persons experience.

In a very special sense, they require affirmation of their uniqueness and self-worth so they can accept themselves wholly—with emotions and feelings on a wide range, with virtues and faults, with highly desirable and less desirable behavior patterns.

This affirmation leading to self-acceptance comes from a variety of sources. In work situations objective measures of productivity help an individual gain affirmation. Emotionally healthy persons maintain inner standards of efficiency or appropriate behavior. Pride in achievement and norms of behavior serve in affirming the self-worth of the individual. But the major affirming force comes through reactions of trusted companions. For persons in work and career situations, confirmation of personal identity and self-worth may be given by superiors, peers, subordinates and others with whom trusted contact is made. Then retirement comes and those who have provided affirmation are no longer available because the individual is no longer at work.

The wife whose career has been home and family has received affirmation through success in the home and from friends of long standing. She now moves with her retiring husband to another home in a different place. Children, now married, are distant and friends have been left behind. A number of affirming forces are no longer as available to her. She may face a lonely unsatisfying period in life in a place pleasing mainly to her husband.

If the couple can now, through long and open discussion of past and present problems, past relations and new relationships needed under the changed conditions of retirement, develop a more deeply sharing companionship, each can help affirm and support the sense of self-esteem and self-worth in the other. Each, feeling the trauma of being pushed outside center stage of society as retired persons, can easily feel losses in self-esteem. One task of a full companionship lies in giving needed affirmation to the other partner.

People need people for affirmation, for the warmth of human contact, as a preventative to loneliness, for support and help, for stimulation and growth.

In Martin Buber's "I-Thou" relationship he indicates how each person is responsible for the growth and development of the other, as well as for the self. No person can be a healthy "I" without the support of a "Thou."[1]

The late psychologist, Abraham Maslow, listed at the apex of human needs that of self-actualization—of reaching as much of one's potentials as possible, and of developing oneself to as complete, whole and open an individual as could be achieved. Self-actualization should not cease at retirement. All have the possibility of continued growth emotionally, mentally and in maturity. Retirement is a time when, with the reduction of external demands, individuals may explore their own motives, emotions and beliefs. If greater wisdom is

---

1. Martin Buber, *I and Thou*, translated by W. Kaufmann (New York: Scribners, 1970).

supposed to be a factor of increased age, then retirement can be a period of increased self-actualization in terms of knowledge and awareness of oneself. Being oneself, knowing oneself, being spontaneous, being honest with oneself and others, being open with others, interacting with others to aid in the growth of both may all be self-actualizing goals more reachable in retirement because conformity pressures are lessened.

But if retirement is viewed as a reward for past accomplishments and with no further self-enriching and growth goals in life to reach, stagnation of initiative and further personal development may occur. In parallel marriages where marital and interpersonal conditions prevent encouragement being given for continued self-actualization be either partner, such stagnation may more readily occur.

Hence, a second major task of regenerated or developed marital companionship is that of encouraging and supporting each other toward increased self-actualization. The saddest and perhaps most common of marriages exists when neither partner thinks the other can continue to grow.

Both partners, as Buber's "I-Thou" relationship indicated, bear the responsibility for helping, though not forcing, the self-actualization of the other. As new richness is developed in either, both may benefit. But the most painful of marriages occurs when one continues to grow while the partner stagnates.

Life-force, the strong desire to live, be active and responsible and survive, is extremely needed and important at retirement when many social and physical agents are pushing toward a loss in such forces. Too many individuals live within limits far below their potentials. They succumb to habits and patterns of thinking that inhibit growth and often lead slowly to self-destruction. They allow their "flame of life" to dwindle. Some cease to maintain the fierce urge to succeed in whatever goals the present circumstances of life suggest. Some perceive retirement as a time to drift without goals.

Those who can set and hold to new goals may feel a rejuvenation of spirit. Such enhanced vital force, as all physicians know, plays a major role in fighting illness. Despair, stress, depression, emotional distress, and unhappiness lead toward illness and debilitation.

So a third major task of a regenerated marital companionship is that of each partner encouraging and helping the other maintain this vital life force against the temptation to allow retirement to deactivate the person. Seeking ways together to continue to find joy in living rather than apathy and despair is a function of an effective companionship.

There are many other benefits accruing from a full and open companionship—the pleasure of sharing important decisions, the opportunity to exchange ideas and feelings, the joy of comradeship in joint endeavors, the opportunity to receive honest reactions to one's behavior that are not punishingly motivated, the feeling of being accepted and respected, and the warmth from being cared about.

Barriers to the Development of a Full Companionship

Many partners in a marriage carry hostility toward the other, long-held and usually expressed obliquely, combined with feelings of guilt for holding such hostile feelings. The guilt tends to prevent the full expression of the hostility save in occasional angry outbursts. Consequently it is difficult jointly to work through the causes of the hostility—the perceptions of the true motives and behavior of the other partner and the mixture of emotions and motives within oneself. With such covert or overt hostility upon the part of one or both partners, there is little motivation to seek a better companionship. To do so both partners would need to be willing and able to uncover the hostility in a non-punitive manner, discover the causes as objectively as possible and seek solutions for an improved companionship.

Because of the difficulties, and because the couple may be unaware of the values of a deeper and fuller companionship, they prefer to "let as many sleeping dogs lie as possible," and continue to live through the marriage as they have done before.

Long years of insufficient and inadequate communications stand in the way of developing an improved companionship. Patterns of casual conversation maintained to prevent as much discord as possible become fixed and neither partner considers tampering with the patterns. Feelings and thoughts remain private unless controversy intervenes to cause an abusing explosion. Each partner essentially walks alone, clutching feelings and reactions tightly, or expressing them in harsh and fighting ways. This pattern of casual conversation and punishing attacks creates a barrier to developing, through prolonged, open, nondefensive discussion, a new type of companionship. Too many years of misunderstanding and ineffective communications have existed. Thus, regardless of the benefits, the generation of a new companionship occurs only infrequently.

(3) Stereotypes, long held and reinforced socially, about a "woman," a "man," a "wife," and a "husband" can easily prevent the development of a full companionship. At retirement time with its different conditions, each partner needs to be perceived and accepted by the other as a *person*. Dissimilarities can be viewed as complementary but equal. Accepted as oneself, rather than as a set of characteristics supposedly belonging to one sex or one role, makes "being listened to and respected" possible. When stereotyping continues, what is heard by the listener is what is expected of "that kind of person."

Rigid role boundaries build barriers to open communications. The generation of a full companionship calls for the open examination of stereotypes and their elimination.

(4) A pattern of dominance and submission between partners serves as a block to the development of a full companionship. With one partner accepted over a long period as superior and the other as inferior, with one expecting and demanding and the other submitting, it becomes difficult for a jointly developed companionship to become possible. The dominance-submission pattern is frequently so subtle and has endured so long that both partners might deny its existence at retirement—the one because it has become habitual and the other because to admit its existence could damage a fragile relationship with no expectation of successful rebuilding. Any such "tilt" situation leads to concealed thoughts and feelings. Yet the building of a full companionship of equal persons requires the elimination of dominance-submissive patterns of relationships.

Developing a Full Companionship

Married partners frequently assume they know each other thoroughly. Unfortunately at retirement this assumption keeps partners from seeking to learn those parts of the other that the previous rush of time and circumstances prevented them from knowing. Sometimes the shock of finding suddenly and unexpectedly different aspects of the other's behavior creates marital turmoil and discord. Before retirement each partner sees the other for only a brief time during the working day. Each is occupied with his own roles and activities. The wife "knows" her husband in the nonwork portion of his life. She does not "know" his behavior with others in the work environment. She hears only his perceptions of that slice of his life.

He, in turn, does not know her in many activities of the day. He only hears her account of the children's behavior, her confrontations with tradespeople and how she behaves with other women in social situations.

Over the long preretirement years of routine, relationships becomes established and fixed. Each spouse performed certain tasks for the other, met and made certain demands on the other, and had certain experiences in common. But much time was left in which each mate carried out different responsibilities, had separate experiences and held different relationships with other persons. Expectations built from these "together and separate" existences could cement the beliefs that each "knew" the other and that retirement would bring little change in their relationship. These beliefs obviously do not consider the great changes retirement customarily brings nor the possibility of greater time spent together under new circumstances.

These beliefs serve as a deterrent to a full companionship. They provide no cushion of understanding to enable either partner to cope effectively with the shock of discovering quite different behavior patterns in the other.

Getting to know each other requires that the couple assume, both just before and during retirement, that conditions are more than likely to be very different with possible emotional consequences, and that the reactions and behavior of each or both may be very different than they were before. The first action step, if this assumption is thoroughly accepted, calls for the partners together to re-examine the image each has of the other. Is this image based on some long-past experience? What discrepancies does the other perceive in the image?

What are the premises upon which images have been built? Past occurrences? Stereotypes about masculine and feminine abilities with superior-inferior labels attached? Expectations that certain duties and decisions must be held by the husband while other less important and menial ones are within the limits of the abilities of the wife? How fixed and previously unexamined are these premises?

What buried hurt and hostile feelings were created? To what extent have inadequate images adversely affected communications between the two? What ideas and feelings have been withheld? These images and the bases upon which they have been constructed need joint examination so each may know the other better and a more complete relationship created.

Getting to know the other requires careful listening. Complete listening calls for concentration and attentiveness in order to "hear" the various messages coming from the sender—hearing the music beneath the words, the feelings behind the words, the things unsaid but implied, the part withheld. Such listening does not occur when thoughts are partially on oneself or on responses or reactions to be given.

Listening is a form of encouragement to urge the other to send the withheld portion of the message and to continue. It is a form of reassurance that the speaker is truly being listend to—something everyone desires. Listening requires receptiveness—not necessarily agreement with the messages sent. In essence listening says, "I really hear you."

Receptivity through listening conveys respect for the other person and is so heard. Incomplete, impatient, inadequate listening is demeaning to the other partner. Such listening says, "You are not worth truly hearing." The first statement may well be a probing of the willingness of the other to listen. If receptivity is felt, the basic message may then be forthcoming.

No one can come to "know" another person without careful listening. If all the messages conveyed in the one statement are inadequately heard, full knowledge of the other is not secured. Incomplete listening causes the message-sender to withhold further information.

There are many facial, body and behavioral cues that tell the sender listening is not occurring—the half-opened mouth as if a reply is already formulated before the message has been completely sent, the abstracted look in the eyes, restlessness of posture communicating unconcern, a response showing the message was not heard.

There are many barriers to good listening: previous assumptions the listener holds about the speaker; anxiety to respond, inform, correct, rebut; and defenses against assumed personal attacks or cherished beliefs. A listener can always check listening ability at the end of a conversation by asking the speaker if he felt he had been listened to.

Getting to know another person more fully can be helped by encouraging a first statement by saying, "Tell me more," or "What happened then?" or "How did you feel?" The music beneath the words can be better understood by questions directed at the feelings of the other. "You seemed to me to feel deeply about the incident. What caused you to feel so strongly?" Such a question can both help the first person think through and perhaps understand himself better as well as aid the listener to gain a greater grasp of the total situation and it can conceivably be of help. The listener could even ask further, "I wonder if you really hate So-and-So because of this one incident, or whether other events have occurred, or if some of your own feelings and beliefs are part of your reaction?"

The most unhelpful and destructive action a listener can take is to tell a sender not to feel as he does. Feelings are as real and factual as any thought or bit of knowledge. Being told not to feel as one does changes nothing. The feeling remains. The one being told is demeaned—is said to be wrong. Guilt may be produced and a sense of worthiness reduced. Pretense may occur. The person may agree, untruthfully, that holding such feelings was wrong, although the feelings remain. No learning can result because the person has no opportunity to explore with assistance the basic causes of the feelings. Rejection is felt and the listener has proved superiority is not possessing these feelings.

Coming to know the other person requires allowing him sufficient freedom to be and feel as a separate person. Hovering over him, smothering with over-protection removes the certainty of identity. Allowing the other person to be and feel different without feeling inferior, encourages him to feel a complete person. Efforts to pressure another to behave, think and feel as one does, denies personhood. The result of submission is often hostility, phony agreement, withheld information or conflict. Hostility may be expressed in indirect and unassailable ways.

Be open. Being open encourages the other person to be open. Being open in sharing thoughts and feelings is an effort to become closer psychologically or to explore and solve interpersonal prob-

lems on the basis of equal to equal and with a minimum of misunderstanding, conflict and hurt. Again, being open does not mean
that all sharing should be calmly logical nor that feelings should be
inhibited or unexpressed. But when the goal is closer understanding
and joint problem-solving, emotions, as very much part of the situation, need to be expressed. Two examples may illustrate the differences in which some emotions are expressed.

> *Wrong:* "You make me very angry. I can't stand the way you act." The
> response, because this type of open expression of feeling attacks
> the other, is usually:
>
> "You make me just as angry. You always get under my skin with your
> behavior."
>
> *Result:* Conflict with little hope of mutual understanding and with con-
> tinued hostility.
>
> *Better:* "I think we have a real problem to work on together. I felt a
> surge of anger after our last interchange and I suspect you did as
> well. I don't want to keep this anger bottled up inside me and I
> doubt if you do either. To begin with, I accept my share of respon-
> sibility for what happened. Maybe then I can tell you exactly how
> I'm feeling and you won't think I'm putting blame on you. Then,
> if you could tell me how you are feeling, we can get down to find-
> ing out what is wrong and what we can do about it."

This method neither attacks nor places all blame on the other. It
acknowledges equal responsibility. It asks for problem-solving after
each has been able to get his feelings known to the other. It does not
invite conflict.

Obviously the second approach is far harder to accomplish, given
the pent-up feelings in both individuals. Also, the second person
must accept the invitation of the first person—the sender—so that
feelings can be aired and examined without any necessity of proving
one or the other "right." If the sender's invitation is rejected but the
sender resists launching into an attack, progress still can be made.
What the sender should do is continue to express his share of the responsibility for the incident, saying, "What did *I* do to cause you to
do such-and-such?" The sender must continue to treat feelings as
facts to be shared and refuse to play a one-upmanship game. If this is
done, a couple can learn to express and share feelings without attack.
Because it is difficult to separate behavior from the individual, a

couple needs to work through immediate problems before immediate anger settles into fixed dislike between them. If individuals could finally say, "I can see where my behavior (not *me* but *my behavior*) contributed to our difficulties, and now I think I can change this behavior (not *me* but *my behavior*)," joint problem-solving of emotional problems in relationships could occur.

Getting to know the other partner helps in getting to know oneself. Put in reverse, getting to know oneself helps in understanding the other person. That is how the development of a trusting companionship provides a mirror in which both can see themselves through another's eyes.

Knowing, being aware of and accepting oneself reduces fear that creates rigidities of behavior and belief, anxieties leading to agreement and conformity to others' opinions, terror of dislike and rejection, lack of self-esteem and concern about needless internal worries. Knowing oneself frees one to listen and understand others. One way of coming to know oneself better is to use the mirror of trusting companionship through continued open discussions.

The mirror will not work if one is only seeking praise, a pat on the back, reassurance, and the other gives false and untruthful reassurance.

Feedback from the mirror of a trusting companionship need not always be critical. Frequently the reporting of perceptions and outside data, if correct, about the behavior and accomplishment of one can erase self-doubt and reaffirm internal beliefs. But if feedback is given falsely, exploration into further self-knowledge is blocked.

Praise the individual knows is unwarranted only demeans by saying, in effect, that the individual is perceived as too weak to hear the truth, but must be constantly bolstered. Criticism the individual recognizes as motivated by the desire to hurt can only create counter-hostility.

Possessive Versus Caring Love and the Effect on True Companionship

Possessive love controls and demands a price from the other person for being loved. Possessive love smothers and demeans, regardless of the perceived motive, because to be possessed is to give up part of oneself.

The poetess, Sara Teasdale, described in two lines the essence of possessive love:

No one worth possessing
Can be quite possessed.[2]

Possessive love is self-oriented and seeks self-gratification. It may grow from feelings of inadequacy and fear of losing the possessed one, so the clutching and demanding increases. Whatever its roots, whether from self-doubt, self-dislike, or fear, its purpose is to satisfy oneself without consideration of the well-being, growth and self-respect of the other. The result is conflict, emotional distance and surreptitious escape or submission. No result leads to a healthy, open companionship. Being possessed weakens and demeans one as a person.

Caring love does not demand compensation for loving. It does not demand the other person give up identity, uniqueness as a person, self-respect and a feeling of self-worth. Caring love permits freedom and aids in the other's growth as an individual. Caring love, asking no price in return and making no demands that control the other, is based on self-respect and respect for the other individual.

Only from caring love can come the acceptance of the other and the openness of sharing that can help create a full companionship that validates each in personhood and self-worth.

Building an Openly Sharing Companionship

Four steps are basic in creating such a companionship:

1. *Creating trust.* Trust grows when each partner recognizes the other is honest with himself as well as open with the mate. When rationalizations and excuses are not constantly present and when each mate can say, "I hadn't stopped to realize how my words (actions) would be perceived by you." Or, "I guess I hadn't realized what some of my motives were." Or, "I wasn't in touch with all my feelings, so I didn't think about how I would come across."

   Trust grows as each partner feels the caring from the other. Caring, as previously discussed, is perceived as unselfish concern for the other person, nonpunishingly expressed.

   Trust grows as each partner realizes he or she is fully accepted as a person having self-worth, a separate identity, and contributions to make worth being heard.

2. Sara Teasdale, "Advice to a Girl," in *Collected Poems* (New York: Macmillan, 1966).

Trust grows when both partners feel free to be themselves without fear of recrimination.

2. *Feedback-creating a mirror.* Open and honest companionship, as has been said, creates a mirror in which persons may see themselves as others perceive them. Feedback from one to the other is the process of the mirror. There can be many kinds of feedback ranging from correctly rewarding comments to helpful information and corrective reactions. For example:

"I don't believe you really feel the need for praise, but I'm not certain if you realize how truly meaningful what you just said and did were to me. They helped me to know how deeply you care for me and they also unlocked any hesitancy I had to be open with you. In addition, and certainly of equal importance, they helped me greatly in understanding myself better."

"I don't believe you realize how irritated I become when you repeat the same statement two or three times. Is it because you don't believe I understand you the first time, or is it a habit? Maybe I don't signal properly that I'm listening."

"It seemed to me that in your brief talk with John you were almost asking for a fight. You know better how to handle such situations. Had something caused you to feel angry? I sensed that John heard anger in your voice and that's why he didn't say anything more. Maybe you weren't aware of what he and I were sensing."

This feedback could bring such a response as: "I didn't think I wanted to start a fight, and I guess I didn't realize how strongly I spoke. Probably I wasn't aware of how angry I was. Anyway, thanks for the help. I'll try to talk it through with John when I see him."

3. *Self-awareness and self-acceptance.* An openly sharing companionship requires both partners to have sufficient security and self-acceptance to avoid self-preoccupation so there can be acceptance of the other. Only when partners have self-liking and self-acceptance can they feel free to be honest with themselves and open with each other.

Self-respect and internal security tend to create willingness to discuss rather than argue.

4. *Checking effectiveness.* A healthy companionship does not exist or continue to exist automatically. Maintaining such a companionship requires effort as does its creation. Hence a couple, having built an open companionship, needs to review its effectiveness from time to time. Such questions as the following can be helpfully asked:

a. Have our communications been as free and frequent as before? If not, what has happened?

b. Do either of us feel that thoughts, experiences and feelings have been withheld lately? What has been the cause?

    c. Has either of us lessened in our listening to the other lately?
       Why?

    d. Do we seem to enjoy sharing outside experiences as much as
       before? What has happened?

    e. Has our communication drifted into casual conversation? Has
       this begun to inhibit either of us?

Chapter 6

Communication

Effective communication is basic to the development and maintenance of a healthy companionship and a renewed and re-energized
marriage. Because of the importance of effective communications,
even with its complexities and difficulties, individual emotional barriers, and uncertainty of the motives of the other partner, almost any
couple can benefit in their companionship by a careful examination
of their pattern of communications. How complete and open is it?
How caring or controlling? How understanding or distorted? What
degree of hostility is present?

Communication obviously has many purposes and uses. Whatever
the purpose, the result has much to do with the continuing relationship of those communicating because emotions and motives underlying words and behavior are inevitably part of what is communicated. Communication, thus, is fundamental to the formation and
continuance of any relationship. It can enhance caring and love or
breed defensiveness, distance and conflict.

Individuals seek to connect with other persons through the communication process. An act of communication may indeed be a
probe to discover the kind of relationship that can be established
and, in fact, may by its effectiveness help to produce a desirable connection. Who has not experienced the flood of warmth and happiness when a statement brings a response indicating understanding
and emotional sharing?

One man said, "That tree is dying." The other responded to the

159

message underlying the statement. "I feel sad, also. Drinking in the beautiful greenness of trees fills me with pleasure." The tone of voice of the first man became warmer. "Gee, I'm glad to find someone who feels as deeply about trees as I do."

A connection between two persons has been made that could lead to a deepening companionship. The first person made a short factual statement that did not force the other to respond and left the door open to whatever response the other wished to make. The other man, hearing and responding to the deeper message, answered the probe. The first man could now respond with equal warmth and with a realization he was heard on a meaningful level. A human connection was begun.

Perhaps a small example, but one containing the dynamics of an effective communication leading to a caring human connection. An innocuous statement is made, but one holding a deeper message if heard. The other listened, seeking to guess the basic reason for the statement. Hearing the feeling about trees and nature, and sharing the feeling, he could respond to the underlying message rather than the surface statement. The initiator of the conversation, happy to find himself listened to and understood, could then respond with an implied invitation for further relationships.

Or who has not felt pleasure in a companionship containing dialogues of ideas and knowledge nonarbitrarily and nonpunishingly exchanged?

One says, "I find———to be very important." The other responds, "I also am aware of the soundness of your statement. In fact, it has led me to think of a number of implications the point raises. Have you considered these and do you see other ones?"

The first speaker says, "I hadn't thought of those. Now that you suggest them, I can begin to see many other avenues to explore." Minds meet without the need for rebuttal, but with each challenged by the other to consider new ideas. An intellectual companionship has begun opening the door for them to sharpen thinking and to learn new ideas and approaches to a subject.

Sensitive communication brings connectedness between individuals, whether on a feeling or an intellectual level. Healthy human beings have strong needs to form warm and meaningful connections with a number of other persons. Others, less healthy, may set up bastions to making connections through anxiety and insecurity, even while desperately needing associations with other humans.

Through such connectedness individuals can know the deep joy of sharing feelings and thoughts without fear of judgment or rejection, of being accepted and affirmed as worthy persons, of being aided in self-awareness through caring feedback.

Unfortunately, even in many marriages, this kind of close bond is not common. Too many communication patterns create distances between individuals. Each partner is guarded. Fear, defensiveness and hostility inhibit more complete sharing of thoughts and feelings. Openness and full expression of warmth is checked by the uncertainty of reciprocation.

The result is partial loneliness and the belief one is not understood. While no healthy person can be "an island unto himself," most people experience more internal loneliness and withdrawal into self than is necessary or desirable.

So, at the risk of repetition, open, sensitive, effective communication, whether verbal or nonverbal, should be underscored as the medium through which the richness of honest, warm, trusting and helpful connectedness between two individuals can occur and be maintained.

Caring is considered here to range from the acceptance of another human being as worthy to be heard—rather than reacted to by quick stereotypic judgment—to the deeper caring of another based on a fruitful companionship. In this sense, caring, as opposed to love, is equated with respect for another human being. It is an important ingredient in effective communications. If a person cares, in the meaning given here, then listening for the multiple messages can occur with patience, attentiveness and sensitivity. Listening, on the other hand, is all too frequently "hearing" a few words while silently considering a rebuttal, a defensive statement or a punishing rejoinder. In such situations the hearer makes assumptions about what the other is saying or going to say and waits restlessly for the other to stop speaking in order to respond.

Sensitive listening seeks to hear feelings and motives, as well as words, to determine the most helpful response to the other within the boundaries of one's own integrity. Listening, in this sense, is an ability difficult to develop. But when it is present, the other person is encouraged to make further efforts to communicate. When it is not present, the other person is aware of not being heard and further attempts at communications are inhibited.

Listening, resulting from caring for others, communicates back that the person is being heard on meaningful levels of feeling and thought. Being listened to affirms the dignity and worthiness of the person. Not being listened to demeans and leads toward the lessening of self-esteem.

In marriages in which an open sharing companionship has been established, full listening occurs. When listening is inhibited by preoccupation or emotional or physical upset, the openness of the companionship allows the speaker to make a second attempt to communicate, or to remind the other to listen without fear of lasting anger or buried hurt.

Sensitive and patient listening is a dynamic way to increase communication. Such listening signals empathic understanding and suggests probing responses that encourage and deepen further communication. It does not halt the communication.

For example:

"I had a fascinating time today," one partner says.

"Good" is the response.

Result: Communication ceases, but several messages have been sent by the listener inhibiting further communication.

1. I'm not particularly interested in your day.

2. I'm bored by your long-winded stories of inconsequential events.

3. I have my own thoughts and don't wish to be bothered. All these possible messages leave the original speaker angry or humiliated or demeaned.

As it could have been:

"I had a fascinating time today."

"The enthusiasm in your voice tells me it must have been very special and exciting. Tell me about it." (Reporting data signifying listening really took place, because not only words but feelings were heard. This is rewarding to the original speaker.)

Result: Messages sent:

1. I'd like to share in your enthusiasm.

2. I care about what is important to you.

3. The report of your experience might open a number of avenues of joint remembrance or information I might add.

These messages create warmth and a desire to continue to share.

Sensitive and multiple-level listening and encouraging responses create communication leading to reaching out and connecting with another to form the open companionship so rich in pleasure, important for individual growth and basic to good human relationships.

Communications Patterns Dysfunctional to an Open Companionship and Marriage

Instead of a communications process building a caring, trusting and open relationship and companionship affirming the worthiness of the individuals and creating self-liking and self-acceptance, too many couples develop and harden relationships that are painful and destructive. Under-communication results. Messages are misunderstood and only hostile and punishing feelings are heard. Clashes, crises and problems occurring throughout the marriage remain unsolved and leave partners bloody and bruised and convinced that the particular problem area should be avoided. Nothing is cleared up, feelings are buried and defenses are built against future troublesome interactions.

Instead of messages encouraging sharing, openness and trust, phrases such as the following typically occur:

"You should have _____."
"Why didn't you _____?"
"I've told you time and time again that _____."
"If you would only _____."
"Why do you interfere in _____?"
"You drive me up the wall when you _____."
"Why don't you ever listen when _____?"

Such comments create defensive reactions, guilt, and reduction of a sense of self-worth. With retirement these patterns become more painful and destructive, because each partner now has less opportunity to escape from the other.

Stereotypes and Their Effect on Open Communication

Having perceived each other as "woman" and "wife" and "man" and "husband," it is increasingly difficult to perceive the other in the new light of "person." The stereotypes clog the communications channels. Sometimes stereotypes are used to demean the other. The wife asking her husband questions she knows he is unable to answer attacks his masculine image. "Just like a woman" becomes a put-down.

Stereotypes, habits, expectations built up over time motivate the words spoken or not spoken. They can cause small hostilities to grow into larger ones. Acceptance of stereotypes and assigned roles, with attached perceptions, makes it increasingly difficult to know the real person. With retirement, the lack of understanding of the other individual, accompanied by reduced communication and emotional barriers between the two, create bigger problems.

When communication is inadequate, feelings are kept hidden and each person feels misunderstood. Because previous problems were never thoroughly explored and solved, ineffective ways of relating to each other become customary.

Making the Other Over

In efforts by one or both partners to "make the other over" communication channels become clogged with resentment and unacknowledged resistance. In the name of love, as compared with caring, many pressures and actions hurtful to the other are committed. Sometimes both husband and wife spend much of their marital life in trying to change the other to fit one mate's image of what the other should be. These attempts seldom succeed. They may succeed in getting partial conformity, but only at the cost of hostility. The husband may intimidate his wife until her behavior in his presence satisfies him, though her inner self-pride and self-esteem have been damaged. The wife's constant nagging may bring about her husband's reluctant compliance at home, but he'll exhibit different behavior away from home.

A distinction needs to be clearly made between the futile and destructive efforts to "make the other over" and being helpful through support, caring suggestions or feedback when the other desires help. In the first case, the change is decided upon by one mate and imposed on the other. Naturally, resistance and hostility result.

In the other situation, the person makes the decision to change and grow and actively solicits help from the mate. The process of when and how to be helpful will be discussed in a later chapter.

From idealized memories of parents, from romantic reading, from dreams of the perfect individual of the other sex, persons develop an image of what one's mate should be like. Then comes marriage to an ordinary individual who cannot possibly fit the fantasy. The situation is ripe for endeavoring to remold the husband or wife to fit the fantasy.

A covert tug of war exists with each partner finding aspects of the other to change or correct. Each feels picked and pulled at, not quite adequate and not fully understood. Endeavoring to make one's mate over is essentially saying the mate has faults and should feel guilty. Feeling guilty usually brings feelings of resentment and hostility. When one is made to feel guilty and inadequate, one's self-image is assaulted and the process of self-dislike and feeling of futility begin. Endeavoring to remake someone is typically a destructive act. The most precious possession one can have is acceptance and a liking of himself. When these are attacked, the very personhood of the individual may be hurt.

The wife who said, "If only my husband would see me as a human being and not as a possession," was verbalizing her resentment in living a role to satisfy her husbnad, but not herself.

Frequently partners are obsessed by *what others will think*. Feeling insecure themselves and fearful of rejection, they are constantly on edge lest their mates be and behave in a way the outer world would disapprove. So great is their anxiety that their partners "show well" that they correct every minor flaw they perceive. At first their efforts to change their mates are made in private, but as these fail, corrections are made in public. "Don't do that," or "I thought you promised not to ____ " or, "What will these people think?"

Not only have they embarrassed their partners, but their tensions and anxieties have made others feel uncomfortable. Equally discomforting to others is the tendency of the obsessed partner to explain or apologize for a mate, even before the mate has said or done anything. "Don't mind if Sam doesn't talk. He never does," is calculated to warn Sam to mind his manners.

Obsessively finding flaws in the other indicates not only little respect for the other but also little self-respect and self-liking. Self-hate brings insecurity and continuous pain. Often the pain of self-dislike is handled by blaming others.

One wife told us that whenever she and her husband attended a party, she had a great time and interacted easily with others. Her husband, on the other hand, found socializing awkward and difficult. On their way home he would bitterly accuse her of making a show of herself. His punishment of her, motivated by his anger at his own inadequacy, managed to end her evening unpleasantly.

Efforts to make one's mate over, whatever the causes, serve as a detriment to the development of an open companionship. Efforts to make the other over are acts to enforce conformity and subservience of one to the other. With the lack of respect and rejection of one's worthiness, integrity and personhood, one can only bury resentment or feel inadequate with consequent dislike of oneself or of the mate.

Punishing

Punishing remarks and actions are frequent between wife and husband. Sometimes the punishing aspects of remarks are not realized. Two examples illustrate this point.

The staff of a woman's organization is meeting. The president says, "Let's hear from Mrs. Adams first. I know her report will be an interesting one." The other staff members feel put down. They believe Mrs. Adams is the favorite of the president and they feel rebuked as less competent. The president is unaware of the feelings of her staff.

Or consider the case where the husband says, "Here, give me that. You don't know enough, so let me do it." He is reacting to a sexual stereotype and doesn't perceive his remark as punishing.

Usually long experience by a marital couple helps them recognize a punishing remark and to be prepared with a counterattack. Husbands and wives make convenient targets for each other. Only when the punishing remark or action is so subtle that to answer would seem to put the person who is the target in the wrong, is hostility buried until some equally subtle way is found to repay the hurt.

Throughout marriage each partner may have learned the vulnerable areas of the other, areas where a punishing comment can create the most pain, the most guilt and the most defensiveness, leading to an interchange of angry, punishing remarks. The causes of any punishing remark may have little direct relation to the remark itself. Such remarks grow out of momentary hostility, exasperation, interruption, fatigue, or self-induced anger needing a target outside the self. Or they may result from long-held, pent-up hostility, the need to get even for some past event, a desire to prove superiority or any of many long-term reasons.

In any case such remarks as, "You never did listen," or, "Why discuss something you know nothing about?" or, "How many times do you need to be told?" or, "Get to the point," are certain to bring devastating replies from the offended party or sullen withdrawal calculated to leave the one feeling guilty and inadequate.

So each partner learns to be wary about sharing feelings or revealing experiences until there is certainty that there will be acceptance of the comments. Barriers slowly build. Wounds remain unhealed. Self-acceptance and security are damaged. When retirement comes and the need to share feelings is increased, the partners have lost the trust necessary for an open, rewarding companionship. Each escapes the other as much as possible in a variety of ways to avoid the deadly silence resulting from having little to say to each other. In one situation the husband left the home early each morning of the week to go to the club to play golf and cards, returning only in time for dinner.

One way by which one member of a couple continues to punish the other is seemingly to forgive a transgression but continuously to remind the other of the transgression in various subtle ways. The method serves two purposes. It supplies a ready tool to use in punishing the other and it helps the punisher feel superior by being noble in forgiving. The punisher wears the mantle of purity while keeping the other in thrall through guilt.

None of the ways of punishment builds an open, healthy companionship. Instead of punishment there can be the revealment nonpunitively of reactions. To withhold reactions and harbor resentment to prevent punishing the other is to be less than open. Reactions given as helpful feedback serve to release tension and anger in the one and aid the other to perceive the consequences of his behavior or statement. This can be done by two persons having self-respect and respect for each other as part of the maintenance of a healthy relationship. It doesn't require fight or punishment. It is a collaborative working through of a relationship problem.

Refusal to Confront Conflict as a Means of Punishment

Sometimes one partner will react to the actions of the other, either calmly inviting discussion or exploding in anger. The other, instead of engaging in the discussion or exploding back, refuses to comment, looks hurt, pouts silently, cries or walks away slamming the door loudly, indicating anger. These actions do nothing to clear up the emotional attitude. By the one partner refusing to respond, the other partner is left stranded with an unresolved emotional problem and now has guilt added to anger.

Punishment is perhaps the most common way by which individuals and couples, who won't or do not know how to establish mutually respecting and growing relations, develop ineffective patterns of interaction with each other. At the time of retirement, when an openly sharing and mutually helpful companionship is most needed, previous patterns of inadequate communications, antagonisms and distance prevent such a companionship from developing.

As has been stated before in this book, retirement and aging bring new and difficult problems for individuals. This is a time when real caring and sensitive understanding can enable each partner help the other through support and encouragement for further growth.

Demeaning the Other

Stated again, each individual, to be emotionally healthy and secure, needs affirmation of the uniqueness of personhood and worthiness in order to know self-liking and self-acceptance. Individuals receive such affirmation through trusting and caring relationships with another or others. Marriages with respect and acceptance for oneself and each other, with sensitive understanding and with patterns of open and full communication can give such affirmation. But marriages that hang by a thread or are maintained by tradition, social restraint and, at retirement, by the absence of other alternatives, not only fail to provide such affirmation but do much to destroy individual self-liking and the sense of self-worth. The result is often a social disintegration of the basic values of a marriage and, in many instances, the emotional disintegration of the persons involved.

Instead of affirmation of personhood and worthiness, a process of subtle demeaning occurs. Stereotypes about the incompetency of women applied to the wife demean her, prevent her growing and do not prepare her for widowhood. Overprotection under the assump-

tion the other lacks ability reduces the person. Add the many demeaning comments so commonly heard that reduce the person in
front of others and the pattern of nonaffirmation is clearly seen.

Controlling

Controlling the actions of another is frequently a subtle process
hardly recognized by either person. In many marriages each partner
controls the other in small and devious ways or large and more open
ways. Often each expects control as part of the marital contract. Yet
being controlled curtails freedom, places part of one's time under
the domination of the other, and in many instances saps initiative
and inhibits growth. The husband confines the wife to the home,
using age-old role expectations, and expects her to be available. She
may feel greater freedom when he is at work, but retirement reduces
such free time. Demands on her are more frequent and continuous,
creating frustration and feelings of being trapped.

Wives, at retirement, may insist that husbands spend far more
time with them, may discourage male companionship and prevent
recreational pleasures their husbands may desire. In preretirement
time, wives did the shopping alone. Now they may demand that their
husbands accompany them on all such trips.

Obviously any marriage, any partnership, any close relationship
requires some division of responsibilities and duties. Such division
should be collaboratively determined and the partners should relate
interdependently. Controlling, on the other hand, becomes destructive to healthy relationships when the motivation of the controller,
recognized or unrecognized, is to dominate the other, directing activities and curtailing freedom. Controlling behavior, in this sense, is
self-serving and basically uncaring. It is an effort to exert power over
the other without concern for the consequences to the one being
controlled. Resulting from insecurity, feelings of inadequacy, and
self-dislike, such behavior, by reducing and confining the other, attempts to bolster the self of the controller.

Controlling and demanding behavior usually is not recognized by
the person. Covered with rationalizations, controlling behavior is
seen as being helpful, being right, doing good, and not as inhibiting
and demeaning actions toward another.

There are so many ways in which one person controls another—by guilt, by appeal, by tears, by pretended weakness, by illness or by seeking sympathy. Whatever the methods, and there are many more, controlling behavior acts against the development of an open, sharing companionship.

Hence, not only by words but by behavior, by sometimes recognized, but often unrecognized, combinations of motives, and by slowly built patterns of communications, barriers are built, making difficult the development of an open, sharing, equal relationship. Add punishing, demeaning, controlling behavior and verbal interchanges. Add the continuous bickering and nagging used as methods to make the other over. Add self-serving demands. Add insensitivity, making love an imposition and inhibiting true caring. The combination comprises the antithesis of the values necessary for a rewarding companionship helpful to both partners.

Problem-Solving and Conflict-Resolution through Full Communication

In many marital situations interpersonal problems and conflicts are never completely solved and thoroughly cleaned up. Brushed under the rug, given a "kiss and make up," ended with an apology not completely meant, avoided in the future, left with submerged blame, hostility and judgment of the other, scar tissue is the consequence. Complete problem-solving and conflict-resolution require a number of definite steps in the communication process.

1) Emotions felt in almost all interpersonal problems and conflicts, with attendant perceptions of the other, need to be brought fully into the open. The emotions, held by each partner, should be recognized and accepted as the way the person feels—a fact—and not judged as being either right or wrong, or whether the emotion should or shouldn't be felt. The crucial fact that cannot be denied is that each individual feels a certain way.

The expression of feelings in a factual and nonpunitive manner, if listened to and accepted as fact without rebuttal, defensiveness or further anger, serves several purposes: each person knows the fullness of feeling and causes the other is experiencing; each, by releasing feelings to prevent them from smoldering inside and having them listened to openly without reprisal, is better prepared to seek solutions more calmly; and, finding that expression of feeling factually reduces rather than escalates conflict and distorts problem-solving, each has more trust in openness and is ready to take the next step toward solution.

In many instances fear of further conflict, desire not to engage in endless argument or a desire not to hurt the other, causes individuals to allow emotions to build in intensity, like steam in a boiler, until there is an explosion of uncontrollable wrath, producing anger and hostility in the other. Fight, blame and counter-blame, nonlistening, and distortion of facts result in the lessening hope of an adequate resolution of the problem.

While it may be healthy for the individual to get rid of feelings destructive to self, unless the difficulty causing the problem is solved, merely "lancing the boil" is not sufficient. Both must say, "It's good to get our feelings out of our systems so each sees how the other feels. Maybe now we can find out what to do."

But if getting it out of one's system only brings counterattack and further distortion of the problem, catharsis may be counterproductive. Both must be willing to "hear" the other as a way of gaining information vital to solution.

2. The second step in the communications process following the catharsis and interchange of feelings is to attempt together to solve the problem producing the feelings. Blame and apology are not the way. A relationship belongs equally to both persons. Neither is totally to blame and neither is blameless. Each possesses a part of the relationship and each is equally responsible for its maintenance and development. Questions such as, "What part did I play in the situation?" as well as, "What part did you play?" should be asked by both parties.

Normally the solution to an interpersonal difficulty requires some modification in the behavior and self-awareness of both parties. If one alone is expected to admit fault and promise change, a win-lose situation in terms of self-respect has developed. As history has abundantly shown, the loser is the one who feels demeaned and harbors hate. Hence, with each bearing responsibility for the problem and the maintenance of the relationship, each should share in its change and improvement.

A human tendency is to be unaware of one's own behavior and place the blame for any problem on the other, absolving oneself.

Each needs to say, after, or as part of the expression of feelings about the behavior—not the person—of the other, "What did I do to cause you to————?" or, "What could I have done to help the situation?" This recognizes two behaviors clashing—not two persons—and seeks to find how each partner can change.

3. The third step in the communication process for problem-solving is for mutual support to be given to maintain changes in behavior. Each may, from time to time and as occasion arises, reward the other specifically by saying the way the other now acts makes it easier to respond. Maintenance of the changed behavior of the other can also be encouraged by the person reflecting aloud on how much self-change has occurred.

Communication and support should be transactional. One does not merely reward and the other accept. Each supplies specific information helpful in supporting new behavior in the other. Otherwise one is assuming the superior position of giving support to the other without assuming the need of equal support for himself. Change for anyone is difficult. Support from the other is vitally needed. Comments such as the following help: "I have noticed you have not————. This had made it easier for me to change."

4. A fourth step in reducing interpersonal difficulties and supporting change in behavior is required. Either or both persons may slip all too easily into previous behavior patterns. Lest regression, if mentioned, create hostility, defensiveness and conflict, an agreement satisfactory to both parties is necessary. How can each gently remind the other of such a slip without sounding pontifical and righteous? What kind of reminder can be accepted by the other as constructive rather than punishing? A couple can benefit by a careful and open discussion about acceptable ways to remind each other.

5. Even with agreement as to the kind of reminders that won't bring a defensive reaction, a fifth step in building an open, caring companionship is needed. In short, the agreement must be tested in action. Only then will each person know whether and what feelings will be aroused by the type of reminder—guilt, humiliation, anger.

For example, you say, "There you go again. I thought we agreed that————." The result: defensive or counterattack statements. It would have been better if you had said: "We agreed to remind each other of any slip in our agreement. I hope I am doing it right. It may be I am also slipping back to an old habit. If so, I hope you remind me. But just now you seemed to me to fall back into your old behavior, and I felt my old angry reaction mounting, which I don't like to happen to me. Didn't I remind you in a way that is helpful and doesn't cause resentment in you?"

Communication that is open, sharing, trusting, caring, and with equal respect for the other is vital to the type of companionship so important in retirement. Such communication requires tearing down the dysfunctional patterns of relating and communicating of the past. It must be developed thoughtfully, sensitively, carefully and with sufficient time either before or during the retirement period. If this transformation can be accomplished, the rewards in terms of sharing and caring, support during difficulties and the maintenance of a vital force for living can be achieved.

Chapter 7

Helping and Supporting

One of the main contributions of a free and open companionship is the sensitive, caring, effective help and support each partner can and wishes to provide for the other. But providing sensitive and effective help and support is a delicate process requiring trust and awareness as well as receptivity. If ineffectively performed, destructive, resentful and unhealthy results may occur.

First: Anyone seeking to be helpful and supportive should be aware of personal motives.

1. Is it to prove personal superiority?
2. Is it to satisfy oneself irrespective of the consequences for the other person?
3. How helpful can I be? Would someone else be a better helper?
4. Will my efforts to be helpful prove harmful instead?
5. Have I tried to understand the feelings and needs of my mate, or am I imposing my solution on his problems?
6. Is it to prove myself right, even though, by implication, the other person is proven wrong?
7. Is it always to prove I'm right in the eyes of others?
8. Will trying to be helpful weaken or lower a sense of self-esteem in the other person? Weaken or strengthen the abilities of the other to solve a problem?

Second: Anyone seeking to give help and support should be aware of the desires, feelings and motives of the receiving individual.

1. How aware is the helper of the receptivity of the receiver to accepting asistance? Has the helper tested what the other really wants—help, or a "pat on the back"?

175

2. Does the receiver really feel the need for help or support? Or does the receiver need to "feel pain," i.e., become really aware of the need for help before it is offered?
3. Will efforts to be of help be perceived as nagging, applying pressure, controlling?
4. Does the receiver pretend to need help in order to hold the other person? Does the receiver use weakness as a means of control?
—5. Does the receiver feel capable of handling the situation alone and therefore resent interference? However, is the need for change so great that a very delicate and sensitive manner needs to be sought to encourage the receiver to want to change?
6. Sometimes help needs to be blunt and realistic to destroy the fears, phobias and fantasies of the receiver. However, trust needs to be present and bluntness expressed caringly rather than punitively. Furthermore, awareness of what and how much the other can hear and accept should precede the use of this method. The shock of the method must be weighed against possible increased resistance.
7. Does the receiver fear loss of individuality and personhood, uniqueness and independence by the acceptance of help?
— 8. Are there reasons why help is not wanted from the particular helper? Loss of face in the eyes of the helper? Fear of possible continued dependency? Hesitation to admit any possibility of need for help?
9. Does the receiver feel loss of status when the helper says, "Here, let me do that. I can do it better"? Is resentment the result?

Third: Sensitivity to the manner in which help is given determines its usefulness.

1. Sometimes statements of belief in the troubled one's ability to solve the existent problem are most helpful. But understanding of the other's motives and internal strength is a necessary diagnosis before such support is given.
2. Help that does not prevent the emergence of latent strength and ability of the receiver is useful.
3. Help should be given in such a way as to encourage participation by the receiver in making decisions or changes, rather than passively accepting support with little personal involvement. Help that is collaborative—"I'll be glad to help as you do it"—combines help, support and companionship.
4. Offering suggestions of alternatives of action but permitting the receiver to make the decision as to which alternative to take may be a useful and sensitive method of helping.
5. Offering alternatives with the hope that these alternatives will suggest other alternatives to the receiver more compatible with ability is a further extension of this method. But in both cases it needs to be remembered that help forced but not wanted tends to create re-

sentment, guilt, hostility and blocks communication and companionship between partners in a marriage.

6. Probing to see if advice is wanted and will be accepted before advice is given is another way of being helpful.

"As far as I know, there are two choices you can make. Which would you prefer if you decide to go ahead?" "What would you recommend?" "Since you ask, and if it were me, I would choose the second. While it may be more difficult, I think the results would be more permanent. (Being open about the facts of difficulty.) Would the difficulty bother you? (Again, turning it back to the receiver for decision.) "Well, if it is more permanent, I think I can stand the difficulty."

The differences, then, between harmful and useful support and help lies in the motivations of those involved, the sensitivity and skill used, and the relationship between the two. Often, instead of adequate support and help, individuals receive false, incorrect, patronizing or deflating advice.

Support and help at any time requires trust, openness and a caring relationship between the husband and wife. Hence a full and open companionship is supported by the ability of the partners to give and receive support in a way that strengthens rather than weakens, that produces interdependency rather than dependency. In turn, the trust and noncontrolling caring in such a companionship makes possible the ability to help. In retirement and aging the need for mutual help and support possible in a free and open companionship becomes increasingly important. Support and help can be vital in helping each partner to come to terms with retirement and aging, become more aware of oneself, and find greater peace in the later portion of life. But when help is forced and takes the form of pressure, controlling and nagging, retiring and aging can become a disastrous ending to life.

Support and help take place in a number of ways. *Assurance* and *reassurance* are two of these ways. They are similar in many characteristics, but subtly different in others. Assurance may be given without being sought—at least verbally and directly. Assurance may be given by one as a result of misreading the needs of the other. Assurance may grow out of the motives and needs of the assurer rather than from signals given by the person assured.

Reassurance, on the other hand, is usually sought, sometimes unknowingly, although the motives for seeking are usually mixed and not always clear. As a result the motives of the reassurer may be self-oriented and unhelpful to the seeker.

Assurance

There are certain aspects that differentiate assurance from reassurance.

1. Body language cues, often given without personal awareness, signal anxiety, doubt, fear, or hesitation on the part of an individual faced with certain actions or social situations. Nonverbal body postures or facial expressions say, "My ego needs bolstering. I need to have my ability assured." Sensitivity to such cues and the giving of quiet assurance, rather than advice can be tremendously valuable to the recipient.
2. Sometimes body build and postures or facial expressions are incorrectly read as signals for the need of assurance, when, in fact, no assurance is needed or desired.
3. Assurance given when not needed or wanted can breed resentment, feelings of being denigrated or suspicions of being flattered. Trust is consequently lessened.
4. Frequently it is the need and motivation of the assurer to give assurance rather than the wish of the assured to receive assurance. Assuring others may increase personal satisfaction and conviction of doing good, irrespective of the feelings and consequences of the assured. In such cases the assurer hovers over the assured ready to give assurance frequently.
5. Unneeded or too frequent assurance can create dependency in the other to weaken ability to accomplish and thus reassure self.

Being sensitive in an understanding companionship for the need for infrequent assurance that still honors the strength and ability of the other to do for himself is one of the important attributes of such a companionship.

Reassurance

While reassurance is typically sought verbally, the motives of the one seeking and the other giving reassurance are usually complex, mixed and often destructive to the emotional health and growth of both persons.

1. The request for reassurance may not be a request for help, but a call for a pat on the back. If correction or advice is given instead of praise, the seeker is disappointed, disregards the advice, and feels hostility toward the other for not responding as desired.

2. The request for reassurance may be incorrectly heard. The intent, irrespective of the words used, is entirely different. All that was wanted was to be told that the behavior was adequate.
3. The seeker wishes one slight suggestion or reaction to one small part of behavior. Additional reactions or advice are not wanted. When required to listen to far more information than is desired, frustration and hostility occurs.
4. The seeker may wish no response affecting behavior. All that is desired is an expression of warmth and closer relations with the other.
5. The seeker of reassurance may be in a dependency pattern. The seeker is using reassurance as a substitute for personal effort to develop self-esteem. One may become "hooked" on the need for reassurance.

Because the seeker seldom reveals all the various motives, or is unaware of their existence, or communicates poorly, the responder is left in a quandry as to what is really wanted. In addition, the motives of the responder may also be complex and mixed.

1. The responder, with a strong desire to be liked and not certain that any constructive comment will be heard, says, "Everything's fine. Don't worry. You're doing great." The response is misleading and unhelpful if the seeker was looking for more than praise, but the responder has not endangered his image of goodwill, although his help may not be sought again.
2. Sometimes the responder fears the other will be hurt by truthful reactions. Rather than take a chance of destroying a close friendship, the response is bland and comforting if not helpful.
3. If the responder fears conflict and wishes to avoid any tension, comforting reassurance may be given. It would be better, if the companionship is on a trusting level, for the responder to ask, "I'm not certain what response you hope I will give. I'm not very good at giving advice. If you really wish me to be open about my reactions, I'd be willing to, but I would want to feel that our relationship is sufficiently open that I wouldn't hurt it." Such a response is not the easiest way to react to a general question, but it seeks to determine, before responding, what answer the other is seeking and at the same time attempts to safeguard a relationship.
4. The responder may relish the opportunity to give advice and so not bother to sense what response the other really desires. Or the responder may be so motivated by a desire to show off superior knowledge that too much information or too many corrections are given.
5. The responder may sincerely wish to help the other, but in so doing is insensitive to the feelings and desires of the other person.
6. Sometimes the responder feels inadequate in giving helpful reactions, yet feels incapable of admitting ignorance in the area of the

question, and so gives misleading information rather than suggesting other sources of help.

For example: An individual seeking reassurance or help asks, "I've had this pain in my stomach for several days. I wonder if anything's seriously wrong?" Part of his motivation is to be reassured that all is well. The other responds by saying, "Think nothing of it. I am sure it will disappear. I've had the same thing." The response might better have been, "I can feel your concern. Probably it's something temporary, but would it relieve you to see your doctor?"

Reassurance may be very helpful, particularly if it fits into efforts the other is planning to make, and the responder is sensitive to the type of reassurance sought. Reassurance can help in evaluating progress and may encourage further effort.

"Your decision to ——— sounds good to me, knowing you and your abilities. I'll be interested in your progress."

"From what you say and what I've seen, your efforts certainly seem to be paying off. You are as familiar as I am with the plateaus one faces in getting better, and I feel confident that any plateau you hit won't throw you." (Reassurance plus alerting the other to possible plateaus.)

"I've noticed how much difference your efforts have made. I know you are aware of it also, but maybe it helps to know others see it too." (A report of observation that takes nothing away from the person's own assessment and self-esteem.)

In these cases reassurance supported actions planned or underway, did not create continued dependency on the reassurer, and were specific to certain events and behavior rather than being general. Unless the actions of the reassurer were harmful, the reassurance was helpful. Furthermore, the reassurer was careful not to give additional advice. Neither was there reassurance until some concrete plan or action was being taken. The reassurer did what was sought—no more, no less.

Giving Support

Support, either on the action or emotional level, provides still another way of being helpful. Sensitivity to the need for support, but taking care that the support adds to what the individual can do for himself, helps without taking away initiative.

1. "Your idea seems to be a good one to me. Any emotional support I can give that does not infringe on your own strength, I shall be

happy to provide." (Here the supporter is careful to confine the promise to emotional support. The responsibility for action is not taken from the other.)

2. "Knowing you, I feel you can do what you are planning and I certainly support your effort and I hope you take the initiative and go ahead." (Here, again, emotional support takes the form of a stated belief in the other's ability and thus serves as encouragement.)

3. "I certainly cannot advise you, and I doubt if you would really want me to, but I see two ways in which I might be of help. If you are seeking someone to bounce ideas off of, I'll be glad to help, although I won't have answers. Or I might be of help by raising questions or suggesting alternatives for you to consider. A number of questions have already occurred to me and perhaps they may be relevant to you now."
   "Have you thought of ———?" "What is the next step you would need to take if your first efforts succeed?" "What will happen if ———?" "Who else do you think could help you? Is there any professional aid you might seek?"

4. "Just what is bothering you? I'm not certain, from what you've said so far, exactly where your problem lies. Would you like to take a little more time and give me all the background you think pertinent." (By asking the other to talk further, help was being given in encouraging the other in a deeper diagnosis of the problem.)

Giving Advice

Giving advice is usually the most ineffective way of being helpful. Unless honestly sought with the expectation of use from an experienced or professionally trained person, advice seeking and giving is generally a superfluous relational dance between two persons.

1. The advice-giver experiences an ego-lift at the opportunity to exhibit knowledge or experience. Feeling gratification and satisfying himself may have little relevance to the needs of the other. The object becomes that of stating what "I would do" and therefore "What you should do." This temptation prevents the advice-giver from understanding the needs, expectations and resistance of the advice-seeker.

2. The advice-seeker may have no fundamental intention of following any advice given, but rather attempts to draw attention and seek sympathy for himself to discover how the other will respond, and, perhaps, to build further resistance to change. For example:
   Question: "Should I give up smoking?"
   Advice: "Of course. Evidence indicates the danger of smoking. I've wondered why you haven't done it before. I did, and I know it takes guts to do so."

Consequences: The advice was not wanted. Sympathy was. The advice given was already known by the seeker. No effort was made to determine the resistance the seeker had to giving up smoking. Rather punishment was inflicted by the sentence, "I've wondered why you haven't done it before."

The seeker was "put down" by the statement that "I did" with the inference the advice-giver was stronger than the seeker. The final punishment and put down came in the statement that "it takes guts to do so."

The advice led the seeker to feel hostility toward the other and to strengthen resistance to change.

3. The advice-giver often seizes the opportunity to give far more advice and information than is sought. While this enhances the giver's self-esteem, it diminishes the understanding and acceptance of the advice by the seeker.

4. Then there are the individuals who give advice gratuitously without being asked. Such advice is usually resented and resisted. The purpose of such advice-givers is viewed by the givers as being helpful although the opposite views are held by recipients.

Advice-giving to be effective should meet certain conditions.

1. The advice-seeker needs to be desperately in need of help and fully receptive to considering the use of advice.
2. The advice-giver needs to be experienced in the field of the knowledge sought.
3. If seeking initial advice of a friend, the advice-seeker needs to trust the honesty of the advice given.
4. The advice-giver, before offering advice, should probe by further questioning the causes of the need for help and the receptivity to its use.
5. The advice-giver needs to solicit information from the seeker as to other avenues that have been tried. In this way the advice-giver will not be repetitious.
6. The advice-giver should be sensitive to the kind and amount of advice the other can absorb. Sensitivity as to how advice is given so that it is not punishing or does not increase resistance is needed.
7. The advice-giver needs to place himself in the position of the recipient. Rather than, "I would do this," or, "If I were you," the advice-giver needs to remove the "I" from advice.
8. The advice-giver needs to be aware when reference to another source should be made, rather than giving advice alone.

In an effective marital companionship, advice-seeking and advice-giving should be reciprocal. Each partner should be able to seek help and advice and be prepared to receive. Help should be interdependent—never one-sided.

All these efforts upon the part of either partner in a marital companionship must overcome a number of common barriers to change:

1. "I'm too old to change." This cliche justifies making no effort to understand oneself. Such an attitude is passive, negative and thoughtless.
2. "I've been very successful. Why change now? What should be different about our relationship?"
3. "No one has ever understood me. Circumstances have always been against me. There is no use in trying."
4. "Ever since I've been a child people have tried to make me change in various ways. Now that I'm retired I'd like to be left alone."

Such barriers, among many others, need to be broken down by the person with the help of the other, if an interdependent, effective marital companionship leading to the slowing down of aging is to occur.

Books which may give you more information on helping and changing are The *Dynamics of Planned Change* by Lippitt, Watson and Westley (New York: Harcourt, Brace, 1958) and *Planned Change* by Bennis, Benne, Chin and Corey (New York: Holt, Rinehart and Winston, 1976).

Chapter 8

Loneliness, Aloneness and Privacy

Loneliness is practically universal. All persons know some loneliness at times, whether alone or with others. Those most unfortunate experience loneliness almost all of the time. The cause of their extreme loneliness creates further withdrawal and further loneliness. For them, loneliness is one of the most tragic and debilitating occurrences, both mentally and physically, that may occur.

Aloneness and privacy, while seemingly similar to loneliness, are usually as dissimilar as sickness and good health.

Loneliness

The anxiety, hopelessness, feelings of inadequacy, and depression that exist for lonely persons is, for most, beyond the realm of comprehension. The devastating fear confronting continuous loneliness is difficult to understand even by those who have experienced, as we all do, temporary loneliness. Loneliness is like a cancerous growth that spreads and deepens. Loneliness feeds on itself. Fear of rejection or hurt causes the individual to reject invitations from others or to behave in such a manner that others fail to offer invitations again. So the individual withdraws within himself, feeling ever more lonely but lacking the initiative to extend himself for fear of further rejection.

Loneliness deprives the individual of the necessary psychological sustenance for a healthy, even sane life. Prisoners when placed in solitary confinement suffer frequently what is known as being "stir mad," a psychological consequence of deprivation of human contact.

Loneliness deprives the person of warmth and caring—the emotional medium of exchange between and among individuals. As individuals have the opportunity to offer psychological sustenance to others, so do they receive sustenance in return.

Loneliness, whether caused by fear of rejection or hurt, paranoia, inability to extend oneself so that human interaction warming to the parties can occur, is dangerous to mental and physical health. A child lonely without peers or playmates may readily develop a painful shyness, preventing his ability to interact socially. As the person grows older loneliness may increase, causing a situation impossible to cope with.

Some out of fear push people away before they can be approached in human friendship. They have become sick and their fear outweighs their loneliness. Others in retirement, accustomed to being approached because of rank or status, wait now for others to make the approaches. When this does not occur, their loneliness is mixed with self-pity and the blame of others. Rather than extending themselves, they increase in loneliness. Still others find the consequences of having no goals in retirement to be loneliness as they lack the motivation provided formerly by their work. Those who live alone and are left alone know loneliness to the greatest degree.

Certain foods build a healthy body. Caring relationships with others build the whole person.

Loneliness creates unhappy and often sick individuals. Each person to remain mentally healthy needs to relate closely to others for love, caring, understanding, support, validation of reality, confirmation of the self, stimulation and growth. On the other hand, loneliness creates distorted, closed and shriveled minds. Loneliness depresses. Warm human companionship energizes.

Aloneness

Aloneness, in moderation, is necessary for emotional stability, growth and good health. In moderation, it differs from loneliness in vital ways. Rather than being depressive, aloneness may help to reenergize and revitalize. Walt Whitman said, "I loaf and invite my soul."

Aloneness provides opportunity to become honestly acquainted with oneself. It is a time, particularly at retirement, to look at oneself and one's behavior in terms of the changes retirement brings. Aloneness is an opportunity to mull over feedback from others that, while sometimes painful, may be an aid to growth. Aloneness may provide sufficient leisure to absorb and consider information contrary to what one has strongly believed to be right. Aloneness supplies space for self-reflection and the development and acceptance of self-identity rather than the role-identity imposed by others and work conditions.

Retirement time, when new emotional crises may be overwhelming, requires such self-analysis to bring increased internal strength. At this time, flagging energy needs restoration lest goallessness and despair occur.

But too much aloneness quickly produces loneliness for many. The need for aloneness should be carefully balanced with the need for understanding and helpful companionship.

Privacy

Privacy is similar in many ways to aloneness. Its differences are subtle but vital. Aloneness, through self-reflection, produces knowledge and acceptance of one's identity. Privacy helps to protect the integrity of this identity.

Each individual needs a psychological "turf"—an area where no intrusion is wanted—a space that figuratively says, "Private—No Trespassing." When one partner in a marital relationship dominates and controls the other, privacy to be oneself is less possible. Or when one partner seeks to absorb the time of the other, privacy is invaded.

Thus each member of a marital situation needs to be sensitive both to himself and the other's requirement for privacy as well as for companionship.

Dysfunctional Marital Relationships Versus Marital Companionship

When a marital relationship has minimal communication or contains mutually abusing and punishing behavior, each mate can feel a deadening loneliness while living side-by-side with mutual hostility. Each is encased in a chamber of misunderstanding, conflict and insensitivity. Each can feel alone during periods of minimal communication. Each can seek to be alone, even if depressive loneliness results from the lack of helpful companionship. It may be preferable to time spent together.

But when a truly full companionship has been built by a marital couple, loneliness is prevented and aloneness and privacy respected. Because thoughts, actions and experiences in alone time are shared later, nothing between the partners that would cause loneliness is likely to occur.

Chapter 9

Emotional Survival

How individuals face and cope with the many adjustment exigencies in retirement depends in large measure on how they deal internally, and consequently by their behavior, with the emotional upheavals inevitably to be confronted. Whether they live dull, commonplace or unhappy lives, or fulfilling, self-productive, self-rewarding, happy and growthful periods in retirement thus becomes a matter of emotional survival. How they cope with often unexpected emotional upsets—not in terms of the picture they present to others but within their internal selves—greatly determines the pattern of their retirements.

Thus this chapter, following the concerns discussed in this book, endeavors to suggest various ways individuals may commence to prepare themselves, beginning even in the youthful years of life, to meet these upsets later in life. While efforts just prior to retirement to anticipate potential emotional upheavals at retirement are far better than no anticipation and planning at all, continued growth of the self and the development of inner resources over a longer period tend to make coping with these emotional upsets more effective.

A clear distinction is made between preparation and planning. While both are important, a person does not typically *plan* in youth or in the early and middle periods of adulthood. Retirement lies in the future. Present aspects of living are in focus. But preparation for retirement can and properly should begin in these years. How the person builds his life is important. Does he continue honest self-awareness or indulge in rationalizations, defensiveness and the blocking off of the acceptance of feelings and emotions? Does he continue efforts to increase his internal resources and self-liking or does he stagnate? Does he successfully cope with emotional crises, changes and transitions or does he become depressed and dependent during such situations? Does he increase his ability to socialize in a way to increase self-esteem or does he become withdrawn and fearful of extending himself? Does he maintain curiosity or permit beliefs to become rigidly cemented in neat little boxes? How he conducts his life during youth and middle years determines how effectively he will cope with retirement.

This chapter confines itself to emotional upsets for other reasons. The vast amount of literature, both books and articles, and the growing number of associations and special groups devoted to the problems of the elderly and the aged answer many of the problems potential retirees face. There has been a rapid increase in specific courses and programs in adult or continuing education arranged for the retired—well over five hundred universities and colleges now offer such programs—and the growth of small apartments surrounding a central eating facility, as well as senior villages and condominiums now serve many retired persons. But few of these deal deeply with the emotional problems common to retirement. Preparation for retirement in this area falls into four major categories.

1. Development of the self.
   a. In adolescence and early adulthood
   b. In middle age
      At retirement
2. Growth through interpersonal relations.
3. Marital relations.
   a. The marital contract
   b. Periodic marital reviews
   c. Pre-retirement marital review
   d. Post-retirement marital review
4. The process of maintenance of self-development, growth through interpersonal relations and marital adjustments through retirement.

The Development of Self

In a large sense the preparation for retirement, for being elderly and ultimately aging, should begin very early in life. The degree of inner strength and good emotional and mental health begun early and continued through life helps to determine how effectively the emotional and relational problems attendant upon retirement will be dealt with. That is why the curriculum of educational institutions should include attention to the socialization and mental health needs of students.

Middle and late adolescence is selected as a realistic starting point for preparation for retirement through the development of the self for two reasons. First, individuals are largely disengaged from childhood and yet not firmly attached to adulthood. This is a period when individuals are very questioning about themselves, but most sensitive to the comments and criticism of others. Without help, their questioning may lead them into incorrect self-images difficult to destroy later.

Second, the period of late adolescence is one in which more serious thought is given to life achievement goals, whether in a career or marriage. This consideration and uncertainty about achievement goals is also common to the period of young adulthood. Hence, this is a time when two parallel and interactive sets of goals should be seriously considered—life achievement goals and self-development goals.

One of the most common statements we have heard in the many training groups in human relations and self-awareness in which we have been involved, frequently with adult participants in their middle years, was, "If only I had had this experience earlier. How different might my decisions have been, how better my understanding and behavior now, and how different my life could have been."

For years our staff conducted annual summer training programs for selected groups of college students. On many campuses today learning in self-awareness and sensitivity to others is gained either in special programs or as part of the regular curriculum.

When group training experiences held under qualitatively sound, experienced and professional leadership are not available, there are a number of pertinent and searching questions that anyone in this age bracket can ask which would aid in the self-development so important at retirement.

What kind of a person do I want to be?
How well do I think I am developing toward that kind of person?

Fairly well? Some? Not much?

What do I like about myself and my behavior?

What areas do I dislike about myself or my actions? Do I make any efforts to improve or change? Can I?

Would I like to be someone other than myself? Why? Don't I think I can grow with effort into a person I like so I would rather be myself than anyone else?

When I get very much older—retired or very old—how would I like people to remember me?

What do I think I can do— what deliberate plans can I make—what goals can I set for myself to continue to develop inner strength and rich inner resources?

The Development of Self in the Middle Years

Today there are hundreds upon hundreds of programs in self-awareness—often under different names—conducted by institutions, training organizations, companies and organizations, certain sections of the military, churches and other groups. Not all are reputable nor professionally sound, nor even safe for the uncertain or dependent individual. At first sight it is not always easy to differentiate the reputable and helpful from the useless and harmful because of misleading announcements or hearsay from very dependent persons. However, careful inquiry is possible into the past experience and professional ethics and competency of the program or of the reputation and stability of the sponsoring institution or organization.

A large number of these programs, which range in length from a few days through a week or two, can be of great assistance to most individuals. They may be harmful, however, for those who are overly defensive, rigid and fearful, or emotionally fragile. For many, the sessions help in gaining a valuable increase in self-awareness and self-understanding, in recognizing the consequences of their behavior on others and in gaining greater understanding of the feelings and motives of others. Such gains in self-awareness and understanding of others can do much to free the individual from dysfunctional fears of oneself and the perceptions of others, can aid in the building of internal security and the wholeness of the person, and can accelerate the process of self-development.

The hypothetical training group described in Chapter 4 illustrates how, through professionally skilled leadership, a trusting group can gradually grow in which the participants feel less defensive and more at ease in receiving reactions, or feedback, from other members about their observed behavior. Such feedback from trusted peers leads to greater insight into oneself, often to confirmation of abilities and behavior the individual doubted having, and to the reduction of the Blind Area described in the Johari Window shown in Chapter 4. Many men and women, in their late thirties and forties or even older, are often provided opportunities by their companies or organizations to participate in such programs, either conducted by reputable outside institutions or as part of the on-going training program of their companies or organizations.

For others there are a wide variety of groups open to individuals conducted by educational institutions, churches of many denominations, service and training organizations. The NTL Institute of Applied Behavior Science, a nonprofit organization, with national headquarters in Arlington, Virginia, was the pioneering organization that did much to develop this field some thirty years ago. Inquiries to this organization can help the individual locate available and reputable programs.

Groups of many types, dealing with alcoholism, obesity control, smoking or other addictions, and even certain health programs are present in most parts of the country. While not directly related to the self-development important for retirement, they are based on sharing of problems, and peer reactions in a trusting group situation.

Not infrequently groups are held for couples. While the focus generally is on marital or child-parent relations, individual insights and self-development usually occur.

But for those in the middle years who do not have such groups available or who do not seek to gain in self-awareness or self-development through participation in such groups, again there are many pertinent and searching questions individuals may ask themselves that could help to increase their self-understanding and improve their chances of coping more successfully with the emotional aspects of their transition to retirement.

1. What do I now think, with approximately half of my life finished, of myself as a person?
2. Are there any differences in my inner person as I see myself now than what I visualized myself becoming as a person (not in achievement in career) twenty or more years ago? If so, what are the differences?
3. Has my career or home so preoccupied me that I have narrowed the focus of my interests? Has this preoccupation lessened my in-

terest and concern about the growth of myself as a person rather than of my role at work or in the home.

4. Have my interests in serious reading, the arts, history, philosophy, curiosity about other cultures, and world concerns lessened over the years?

5. Am I more rigid in my beliefs, more judgmental and less tolerant of others, less pliable than I was twenty years ago?

6. How well do I really know myself? How much do I rationalize my thoughts and behavior? Have I taken time to reflect about myself as a person?

7. What do I like about myself? Dislike? What do I do or what is there about me that I dislike? Why? Do I do anything to change my behavior or to remove the dislike? Where and how did I learn to dislike parts of myself? What does this dislike do to my total acceptance of myself? What does it do to my feeling of ease with myself, my sense of peace and serenity?

8. When do I think I stopped growing as far as my inner person is concerned? Why then? What happened? Was it so gradual that I slowly forgot to be concerned with the development of my inner being?

9. Some day I will retire. Many of the outside pressures and contacts with others will no longer be present. What richness is there within me that I can draw upon, or will I be dependent on others for initiative and interest? How well will I be able to live with myself?

10. Looking forward to that day of retirement, what kind of a person will I be if I continue as I am now?

11. What can I now begin to do to increase the development of myself as a person? Of my private, inner person?

The Development of Self Prior to Retirement

Today an increasing number of companies and organizations conduct preretirement training or counseling programs for those employees approaching retirement. Generally such programs deal heavily with financial matters, retirement living and hobbies or second careers, and touch more light on immediate adjustment problems in the transition to retirement. Only rarely do such programs go deeply into the many emotional upheavals and adjustments the potential retiree will face, or the marital readjustments inevitably necessary.

But the day is rapidly dawning when, in groups, one hopes with wives included, the many emotional problems of retirement will be discussed so the individuals or couples will not come upon them suddenly, nor face unexpectedly disappointments in their visions of the future. While some enter retirement as a welcome release from hated work, many have unexpressed concerns, anxieties and even fears—as many have told us.

Caution needs to be employed so that the recognition of the many potential emotional problems does not create more fear and anxiety before retirement than is desirable. That is why group sessions are important. With effective leadership, those approaching retirement can share with others in the same situation the plans, expectations, worries, and submerged anxieties and the group members can find companionship in the commonality of the expectations and anxieties. Given this mutual sharing and concern, information about potential emotional and relational problems, as well as other kinds of retirement problems, can be more easily received and absorbed.

But again, for those who have no access to formal preretirement planning, and for those whose formal coaching does not include reference to the emotional upheavals likely to occur, questions can be raised and thoughtfully and honestly considered in the area of the growth and development of the self.

1. Now that I am about to retire, how understanding am I of myself?
2. Have my attitudes and beliefs about life, about others, about myself become so set and rigid—so stereotypic—that I do not question my thoughts and behavior? Have they become so accepted and set by outside forces and by others that I have had little influence in their establishment? Do I think as others tell or expect me to think, or do I think for myself? Honestly?
3. How well do I understand my many motives? To what degree am I in touch, or even understand my feelings and emotions and their causes? Do I deny certain feelings and emotions my body and behavior obviously express?
4. How do I feel about myself as a person now—not just of my achievements—but of me as a person? What do I like about myself? Dislike? Do I try to hide part of myself because I don't like or approve of that part? Do I fully accept myself as me, without excuse or fear?
5. Do I feel I have grown in my inner person since the middle years? The early years? In what way have I grown? In what way not? If not, what has kept me from developing? Preoccupation with career? Fear of myself and what might be discovered by self-reflection?

6. Now that I am about to retire, how do I think I will enjoy my inner self? Will I like to converse silently with myself? Will I find an inner self worth conversing with?
How much freedom from tension within myself do I expect to find at retirement? How much peace and serenity?

7. Have I continued to read seriously—and not just in my field— over the years? Do I any longer enjoy reading anything but the lightest material? Do I have interest in the arts, history, philosophy?

8. How much curiosity do I have about new thoughts, new areas of knowledge, undiscovered aspects of nature? In comparison with my early years? Have I allowed my sense of curiosity to dry up?

9. What do I look forward to in retirement? What do I fear? What planning have I done about my own continued growth? Do I perceive that retirement will provide leisure to come to know myself better? Or merely to be active?

10. Do I expect to experience any emotional upheavals then? Do I feel capable of understanding and coping with any unforeseen reactions?

11. Do I go to church out of habit or do I thoughtfully consider religious ideas and faith?

Growth through Interpersonal Relations

In Chapter 5 reference was made to Martin Buber's "I-Thou" relationship and how each person is responsible for the growth and development of the other as well as for the self. It is obvious that through life individuals learn, and one hopes grow in improving through interaction with others. One hopes, also, these individuals help others grow in improving ways. But, as various chapters in this book have stressed, being helpful to others in their learning and growth requires a number of conditions—desire to help others learn and grow which does not always mean dictating and imposing solutions (growing things and beings require breathing room and the opportunity for self-initiative and inner movement); a sensitivity to the motives, desires and needs of others; and a willingness to be openly interactive with others. As has been said in Chapter 5, one of the basic values of an effective marriage is the "I-Thou" relationship in which each assists the other in growth.

At any age, individuals can reflect upon certain questions concerning their interest in being helpful in the growth of others and their willingness to accept the assistance of others in their growth. While important at almost all stages in life, such efforts and willingness take on peculiar importance at the time of retirement when many persons are content to remain as they are, with growth no longer seen as necessary or desirable.

1. How desirous are you to assist in the growth of another—particularly a spouse? Too desirous? Feeling impelled to help the other at all costs? Impose solutions?
2. How sensitive are you to the desires, feelings, motives and resistances of the other?
3. How needful to dominate and direct the other? How needful are you always to be right?
4. How well do you listen and hear multiple messages? How accurate is your hearing? Is it distorted by what you want to hear?
5. Can you accept feedback reactions from others without being defensive?
6. How close or how distant—how warm or unfeeling—how friendly or formal do you like to be with others?

Marital Relations

As discussed in Chapter 3, marriages take on new purposes and new adjustments need to be made to meet different conditions. Unfortunately many marriages continue as they were, with only minor adjustments, with persisting inadequate communications and a minimum of sharing, with continuing conflict, hostility and the bickering existing before retirement.

For most marital partners there is little expectation that change will occur. Endurance of a less than mutually helpful marital relationship is all that one could reasonably look forward to at this stage in life.

Just as preparation for retirement as far as the individual is concerned should begin early in life, so should the foundation be laid at the beginning of a marriage for the adjustments needed at retirement so that a new vibrancy in the marriage can be produced at that time. A pattern of periodic reviews and renewals held during the marriage also helps to bring appropriate adjustments at retirement.

The Marital Contract

In our generation marital contracts were not common in the sense that they are today. While the wedding service most of us knew had each of the future partners promise to love and cherish (care), and to

endure the vicissitudes of their life together, nothing was said about
the responsibility to aid the other in developing and maintaining
uniqueness of identity, personhood and self-respect. Nor was anything included about the responsibility of each to assist the other in
growing and actualizing the other's potentials.

The beautiful story referred to in the opening of Chapter 3 of the
contract Barbara and Peter drew up for their marriage illustrates the
laying of groundwork for future years. They had built into their
pledges the ingredients for future marital reviews and for joint decisions concerning further adjustments at retirement.

Periodic Marital Reviews

Marriages in which a process of periodic marital reviews and renewals are present have set in motion a method by which problems
and crises may be solved and amicable adjustments made when new
conditions prevail. Communication that is inadequate and emotional difficulties may be worked through to the release, relief and
satisfaction of both parties. A process has been adapted that can
mean much for valuable changes and renewals at the crucial transition to retirement.

It is naive to suppose that such a renewal and review process will
automatically be effective the first time tried. The development of a
pattern of reviews is a slow and evolutionary process. Blame, defensiveness, anger and misunderstanding are barriers to be overcome. Trust needs to grow till neither party feels the other is deliberately punishing. Miscommunication requires working through
until mutual understanding occurs. Fear of hurt must be dissipated.

The evolutionary process of creating mutual security in a marital
review can be speeded up if both partners are willing to evaluate objectively each effort after the review is ended. A calm evaluation,
looking back at the reviewing process, can disclose places where
misunderstandings occurred, emotional reactions erupted, or the
review became sidetracked into superfluous issues.

Such evaluations can result in ground rules for future reviews—
the best time to hold a review, freedom for either partner to suggest
but not force a review if the other feels unready, agreements to post-
pone if defensiveness or tempers flair or the discussion becomes
stalemated.

Each partner will become increasingly aware of self and sensitive to the other as such reviews prove ever more effective. With caring and trust present, each can feel freer to accept a portion of the responsibility for the conditions leading to the review. Questions for a review are found in Chapter 3. They are merely suggestive. Couples may make up their own lists.

Preretirement Marital Review

The preretirement marital review represents one of the most crucial times for such a review. With retirement inevitably come problems of changed relationships because of living together for more hours of the day. Adjustments to retirement, with the accompanying emotional upheavals each partner is facing, are accentuated and made more emotional if alterations are not made in the relationships between the partners. The husband now at loose ends and the wife with her home invaded face serious problems of living together in addition to the adjustment problems each is already confronting. Each set of problems worsens other sets.

Just before retirement and before the avalanche of emotional blows strike is the important and appropriate time for such a review. Now is the time when husband and wife together—as the hypothetical story in Chapter 3 illustrates—can share expectations and concerns and endeavor both to recognize the problems each will face and to lay some plans for their relationships before the event occurs and anger erupts.

Postretirement Marital Reviews

Previous planning cannot possibly foresee all of the problems and needed adjustments that may occur. At best such preplanning can merely alert both partners that unforeseen problems will occur and to be ready to deal with them before they reach the boiling point.

The same, or similar, process of marital reviews and adjustments that were serviceable earlier in the marriage can be adapted to the present difficult conditions. Thus marital reviews are both necessary and desirable throughout the elderly period in retirement.

Maintenance of Self-Development

Conditions change during the period of retirement as they do during other periods in life. Physical aging slowly occurs; health problems erupt; energy levels slow down. All of these conditions tend to lessen, and even eliminate, desires for self-development, interpersonal relations with others, and even efforts to continue a vibrant, fulfilling companionship in marriage. Such tendencies lead to apathy. Apathy, in turn, leads to physical and mental deterioration. Therefore persons need to persevere to the extent of their ability in order to maintain these three basic conditions for the vital force of living.

There may be some who will be disappointed with this chapter because it does not contain ready-made solutions, quick cures, or surefire methods for handling any and all emotional upheavals that might occur in retirement.

But all that could realistically and honestly be done, based on the description of many of the emotional upheavals discussed earlier in the book, was to make suggestions. In the final analysis each person and each couple must decide whether to do anything but drift, or what could be done either by the person or the marital couple.

Conditions are different for each person and each couple. Each person through living has developed, or has not developed, internal strength and inner resources that will help to determine how emotional reactions will be met. Each person is, to varying degrees, in touch with himself and filled with tension, or has found serenity. These will be the conditions determining how retirement is handled.

Some marriages will have created a fulfilling, rewarding, helpful companionship. Other marriages will experience concealed or open warfare. Again, these provide the conditions determining what will happen in retirement.

All this book could do was to tell our story of what happened to us—what we did—and how we worked together over a number of years of our retirement to discover and cope with the various emotional upheavals we experienced.

We hope this much will alert those considering retirement, those already retired, and those in their middle and early years to look more carefully at retirement than we did.

Index